TWO-MAN AIR FORCE

Two-Man Air Force

Philip Kaplan

Pen & Sword
AVIATION

First published in Great Britain in 2006 by
Pen & Sword Aviation
an imprint of
Pen & Sword Books Ltd
47 Church Street
Barnsley
South Yorkshire
S70 2AS

ISBN 1 84415 177 8

Typeset in 10/12 Times New Roman by
Concept, Huddersfield, West Yorkshire

Printed and bound in England by
CPI UK

Pen & Sword Books Ltd incorporates the Imprints of Pen & Sword Aviation,
Pen & Sword Maritime, Pen & Sword Military, Wharncliffe Local History,
Pen & Sword Select, Pen & Sword Military Classics and Leo Cooper.

For a complete list of Pen & Sword titles please contact
PEN & SWORD BOOKS LIMITED
47 Church Street, Barnsley, South Yorkshire, S70 2AS, England
E-mail: enquiries@pen-and-sword.co.uk
Website: www.pen-and-sword.co.uk

Acknowledgements

The author is grateful for the generous assistance and contributions of the following people whose kindness and consideration made this book possible: Edith Barbato, Gregory Barbato, Malcolm Bates, Isabella Beitman, Peter Coles, Dom DeNardo, James H. Doolittle, Joe Gentile, Bob Godfrey, Jay Godfrey, James Goodson, Hargita Kaplan, Margaret Kaplan, Neal Kaplan, Téa Kaplan, Bruno Masdea, Tim McCann, Judy McCutcheon, Sandra Merrill, Wade Meyers, Merle Olmsted, Steve Pisanos, Dave Raphael, Ray Wagner, Duke Warren, Tom Wheler.

Contents

CHAPTER ONE

Canada

On the evening of 9 August 1941, 19-year-old Johnny Godfrey sat in a train bound from Boston for Montreal. The former athlete, football star and 1940 class president of Woonsocket (Rhode Island) High School was looking for adventure. Much of the world was at war for the second time in that half-century, but the United States had not yet entered the conflict and Johnny was worried that he would miss out on the action and excitement. Earlier that summer, he had tried to enlist in the United States Army Air Corps. Their requirements for aviation cadets, however, included the completion of at least two years of college and his application was rejected. Later, he heard that the Royal Canadian Air Force (RCAF) was urgently seeking pilot trainees. He contacted the RCAF in Ottawa, learned that they required only a high school diploma and decided to enlist. The United States was still a neutral nation and he was certain that his parents would oppose his enlisting in the forces of a country already at war, so he decided to run away to Canada to be trained to fly and fight.

In his book *1000 Destroyed*, Grover Hall, a former Public Relations officer of the Fourth Fighter Group, remembered Johnny:

His parents were prosperous people who were troubled because Godfrey wouldn't go to college and take his higher learning like a man. He was moody, reckless and appeared to be shiftless. His salient feature was his set of darting, gypsy-black eyes. They later proved the keenest eyes in the 4th, disciplined, radar eyes that could spot enemy specks in the sky miles away. But in 1940, they had a restless, faraway expression that reflected Godfrey's maladjustment.

After medical and intelligence examinations at a Montreal RCAF enlistment station, Johnny was sent to Manning Depot, Lachine, Quebec, where RCAF enlistees then began their service. There, he received his uniforms, inoculations and fundamental instruction in Canadian military procedure. A five-week posting followed his four-week stay at Manning Depot to Shediac, New Brunswick, a newly built air station. There, the bulk of his time was spent on guard duty, while awaiting the arrival of the base's new training aircraft. It was during this period that he was summoned to see his Commanding Officer. The CO showed him a telegram. Johnny was shocked to read that the *Vancouver Isle*, a ship transporting his brother Reggie to England with a group of American volunteers serving in the British radar system, had been torpedoed and sunk by a U-boat near Greenland. There were no survivors. Johnny was granted two weeks' bereavement leave, during which he developed a new sense of purpose and dedicated his military service to avenging his brother's death.

At the end of his leave, he was ordered to report to the RCAF Initial Training School (ITS) at Quebec, where he was taught the theory of flight, military tactics, navigation, geometry, Morse code and meteorology. The instruction term concluded with a lengthy written examination, which determined which air branch category trainees were assigned to – air gunner, navigator or pilot. Johnny applied himself to his studies as he had never done before and was rewarded with a ranking of ninth in a class of forty. His chosen category was pilot and his academic performance earned him that reward.

With preliminary instruction behind him, Johnny was posted to No. 4 Elementary Flying Training School at Windsor, Quebec. At Windsor, the trainee pilots learned to fly the Fleet Finch, a slow, relatively forgiving open-cockpit biplane, ideal for initial training. On the morning of his first instructional flight (it was also his first time in an aeroplane), he was introduced to his instructor, a man with a perfect name for his profession – Hop Good. He would become one of the most important influences on Johnny's flying career. Good began by taking his pupil on a brief tour of the aeroplane, paying particular attention to the cockpit and instruments.

In flight, the instructor demonstrated turns, climbing and descending. He then throttled back and pulled the nose up until the Finch gently stalled. Applying left rudder, he forced the aircraft into a spin, which caused Johnny to lose his breakfast over the edge of the cockpit and along the side of the plane. After landing, Johnny had to spend two hours chipping the frozen remains of the meal from the fuselage. Thereafter, Johnny carried a paper bag in his boot whenever he flew. He was eternally grateful to Good for the relaxed yet disciplined manner in which he had been taught.

After a little over seven hours of dual instruction, Johnny was declared ready to fly solo and he approached the test with considerable joy and confidence. Like most neophyte aviators, it was not until he had taxied out and taken off that reality settled on him. In quick succession, his thoughts went from concern for self-preservation to acceptance of responsibility for himself and the aeroplane, to reliance on doing what one has been taught and doing it with as much precision as one can muster in the circumstances. Fly by the book and all will go well, and it did. Before he realised it, his allotted ten minutes of solo flight were over and he set the Finch up for a landing.

Nearly everyone making a first solo flight experiences a particular sequence of emotions. It is an unforgettable event. First, there is excitement in the anticipation. After the take-off, the gut-wrenching realisation comes that your life is now entirely in your own hands. Very soon, it is time to land and that challenge concentrates your mind wonderfully. You are flying, for example, a Piper Cherokee low-wing monoplane in a left-hand-pattern approach. It is a relatively low-powered aircraft with fixed landing gear. You are operating from an uncontrolled airfield and your life is now literally on the line. You begin by looking to see if any other aircraft are in the landing pattern. With the pattern clear, you reduce power to 1,800 rpm and descend to an altitude of about 1,500 feet, flying parallel to the runway you will be landing on, and roughly a half-mile out from it. You are travelling in the opposite direction to that in which you took off. You descend gradually until you reach the point where, when glancing back over your left shoulder, the landing end of the runway is at a 45 angle to you. You're a bit nervous but you ignore that as you apply one notch of flap and turn 90° left, while maintaining your throttle setting and continuing your steady descent. As you come near to intersecting an imaginary line that extends out from the runway, you guide the aircraft through a second 90° left bank onto your final approach and add another notch of flap, still maintaining your throttle setting. At this point you will have descended to roughly 1,000 feet and, if your turn was properly coordinated, you will be lined up on the centreline of the runway and about one mile out from it. With two notches of flap deployed, you are gradually descending at a rate that will bring you over the threshold of the runway at a height of fifty to one hundred feet. You continue descending until you are about fifteen feet above the runway. Now you 'flare' the aircraft by pulling gently on the yoke until the craft is just slightly nose-high. You reduce power to 'idle' and hold the stick and rudder steady as the machine floats gently to the runway. After touchdown, the roll-out begins and you stabilise the plane in its forward motion by gently toeing the rudder pedals. You begin to apply braking. At this point you relax your concentration enough to begin thinking about what you have just accomplished.

With a nearly perfect solo flight behind him, Johnny made impressive progress at Windsor, mastering the aircraft and excelling in his ground school studies. He accumulated eighty hours of flying time and was then offered a choice of continued training in either single-engine or multi-engined aircraft. For a long time he had wanted to be a fighter pilot so he chose the former. With his close friend Joseph Jack of New York City, known as JJ, he was posted to No. 8 Service Flying School, Moncton, New Brunswick. Here, they would learn to fly the North American AT-6 trainer, known as the Harvard by the British and Canadians, and the Texan by Americans. The AT-6 was a great improvement over the Finch. It had a retractable undercarriage, was of all-metal construction, and had a variable pitch propeller and a 150 mph cruising speed.

Unfortunately, Johnny's instructor on the aeroplane was nothing like Hop Good. In Johnny's words, the instructor was 'erratic, overbearing and excitable', just the sort of person one didn't need as a teacher in a difficult and demanding subject. A rebellious streak resurfaced in Johnny and he soon began looking for little ways to irritate the instructor.

At Moncton Johnny and JJ met another trainee, Bob Richards of Newburgh, New York. Richards, Godfrey and Jack soon became the best of friends.

The training at Moncton continued, with considerable dual instruction and night flying. Johnny had his last training flight there on 1 October 1942. Wearing their new wings, JJ, Johnny and Bob graduated from Class Eleven. They were ordered to embark from Halifax, Nova Scotia, for England as sergeant pilots in the RCAF.

The 244 American pilots who volunteered and were accepted to fly and fight for the RAF and the RCAF early in the Second World War were called Eagles. Before the United States entered the war, many Americans had become convinced that their country soon would. Many eager young men yearned to take part in what they perceived to be a great aerial adventure overseas. Their numbers remain in dispute since, in order to circumvent the US Neutrality Act, many assumed Canadian or South African nationalities. The exploits of the Hurricane and Spitfire pilots in the Battle of Britain had captured their imaginations, and the heavy losses incurred by the RAF in the campaign had left it extremely short of pilots. Charles Sweeny, an American businessman living in London in 1940, had noted the growing number of American volunteer flyers coming to England and began organising them into a cohesive fighting unit – the Eagle Squadron.

To assist Britain in that time of extreme need, an organisation in New York City called the Clayton Knight Committee was furtively recruiting pilots in America, so as not to compromise US neutrality. The RCAF would train successful applicants in Canada and then the men would be shipped to England, where they would become members of the Eagle Squadron (later there would be three Eagle squadrons integrated into the RAF). A commercial artist, Clayton Knight, had served as a pilot in the First World War and was later a military illustrator. He was also a friend of the legendary First World War Canadian ace, Air Vice Marshal Billy Bishop, who had persuaded Knight to establish a recruiting organisation in New York to seek and sign up prospective pilots for the Eagles. Homer Smith, a wealthy Canadian and an RCAF wing commander, was appointed administrator of the Clayton Knight Committee. When the United States entered the war in December 1941, the committee had already processed 50,000 applications and approved more than 6,000 Americans for duty with the RCAF or the RAF. Some 92 per cent of the Americans who made up the Eagle Squadrons had been processed through the Clayton Knight Committee.

The would-be Eagles had been gathered from all over the United States. Some were 'all-American-boy' types, bright-eyed and clean-cut; others were not, but all were keen to fly, fight and experience the danger and thrills they anticipated. They were, in fact, violating strict US neutrality laws and might have been subject to serious penalties, including, but not limited to, the loss of their US citizenship if charged and convicted. But so great was their desire to be part of the action in Europe, that they took the risk. If some of them thought that their flying logbooks lacked sufficient hours to impress the Clayton Knight interviewers, they saw no real harm in gilding the lily.

In the early days of the Eagle Squadrons, there were some in RAF leadership circles that viewed these American volunteer airmen as ill disciplined, spoiled and not terribly useful. However, with time and seasoning, the Eagles matured and came into their own, earning the profound respect and admiration of the British.

Chesley G. Peterson, No. 71 (Eagle) Squadron, recalled, 'We were all lying like hell about the amount of flight time we had'.

James A. Gray, No. 71 (Eagle) Squadron, remembered:

It was a curious situation. I didn't have to register for the draft . . . so I didn't have a draft notice. I wasn't trying to avoid the draft, which a number of the chaps were. I had been flying out of Oakland Airport where I soloed, and then went to the University of California where I joined the Civil Pilot Training Program and got myself another hundred hours or so of flying time. About then, word was circulated around Oakland Airport that the British were recruiting for the RAF.

It was sort of *sub rosa* though, because they really weren't allowed to. I had applied to the Army Air Corps and been turned down, and I was really eager to fly with an air force – any air force. So I signed up. I took some exams from a retired Air Corps major who was a medico down in Berkeley. Then, I was assigned to Bakersfield on July 1st, 1940.

Carroll McColpin, Nos 71, 121 and 133 (Eagle) Squadrons recalled:

Most of us were in the 19–23 age bracket. At twenty-seven I was one of the oldest. Each of us had his own reason for joining. Some had washed out of flying school because of the rigid discipline. Others simply could not take the long routine in the US services to become military pilots, when they were already experienced aviators.

For myself, I reasoned that since I had flown most of my life and knew there was going to be a global war, why not start flying for England, a country that needed help and believed in our precepts of democracy, and one that would be our ally soon in any case? I knew America was on the verge of war. When the Battle of Britain started, I decided that I couldn't just stand by and do nothing.

Four schools were set up for training pilots in the United States, as a part of the British Refresher Training Course: at Dallas, Tulsa, Glendale and Bakersfield. They provided 80 per cent of the total of 244 Eagle Squadron pilots.

Jim Gray recalled his fourteen-day voyage from Halifax to England:

It was a boat which used to ply the Caribbean. About five days out of Liverpool, a huge storm developed and our old banana boat just couldn't keep formation with the convoy of some eighty or so ships. The deal was that everyone would keep formation on the slowest ship in the convoy, about eight knots. Well, the commodore of the convoy radioed that everyone was on their own and, for about four days, we were just that – on our own. We were a little nervous because some time earlier, a ship in another convoy had been torpedoed and had gone down with some prospective Eagle types on it. Eleven were rescued but five were lost.

When the new Eagles arrived in London, many were still officially civilians. Most were quickly fitted for RAF uniforms at Moss Bros and given the rank of pilot officer. The majority went from No. 3 Personnel

Reception Centre at Bournemouth, to No. 56 Operational Training Unit (OTU) at Sutton Bridge, Norfolk, and from there to their operational squadrons.

From the start, the RAF was wary of American leadership of any of its squadrons. A British officer, Squadron Leader Walter Churchill, was put in charge of No. 71 (Eagle) Squadron, which was part of No. 12 Group, RAF, commanded by Air Vice Marshal Trafford Leigh-Mallory. Leigh-Mallory had made no secret of his distaste for American fliers in the RAF. Even the Air Officer Commanding, RAF Fighter Command, Sholto Douglas, expressed reservations about the Eagles to the visiting Commanding General, US Army Air Corps, Henry H. Arnold. In the United States, the FBI had been making it difficult for the Clayton Knight Committee to operate and had announced that the US Neutrality Act would be strictly enforced. Then, Prime Minister Winston Churchill intervened on behalf of the Eagle Squadron concept, which the British Air Council was opposing. Fortunately for No. 71 Squadron, it was then transferred from No. 12 Group to Martlesham Heath, as a part of No. 11 Group, where they would see considerable action in the main battle zone. As increasing numbers of American volunteer fighter pilots arrived in England, two additional Eagle Squadrons were formed – No. 121 Squadron at Kirton-in-Lindsay and No. 133 Squadron at Coltishall.

Dominic Salvatore 'Don' Gentile was born on 6 December 1920 in Piqua, Ohio, to Josephina and Pasquale Gentile, young Italian immigrants who had come to the United States in 1907. From the moment when, as a small boy, he had first noticed an aircraft in the sky above Piqua, he had been hooked, completely and irrevocably captivated by aeroplanes and flying. He 'played aeroplanes' and studied books about flying and when he was old enough he began building model aircraft. Like many boys, he was inspired by the legendary aviators of the First World War – Richthofen, Albert Ball, Bishop and Rickenbacker. His dream was to fly and he never wavered in his pursuit of that goal.

In 1936, Pasquale, known as 'Patsy', owned and operated a tavern in Piqua when 16-year-old Don announced his desire to take flying lessons at the Vandalia airport. The lessons cost $15 for half an hour of instruction and Patsy agreed to let Don work for him in the tavern to earn money for the lessons. Don won the respect and encouragement of his flying instructor and was able to solo at the age of seventeen. He soon began to yearn for an aircraft of his own and made life miserable for his father until he finally agreed to help him acquire one.

Late in 1939, with the war in Europe under way, Don was one of the many young men craving involvement. He desperately wanted to become a fighter pilot and a flying ace. His mother and father, however, were equally determined that he would go to college. During his junior year in high school he wrote to, and was turned down by, the US Army Air Force, the Navy and the Marine Corps. All the branches insisted on their applicants having completed at least two years of college. Soon, however, he met an RCAF officer who told him about the Eagle Squadron and the part it was playing in helping the RAF fight the enemy. Don learned that the Canadians and the British were not as interested in the amount of advanced education of their pilot applicants. He also heard about the Clayton Knight Committee and its efforts to find Americans with flying experience to become pilots with the RAF. Some of those who contacted the Clayton Knight Committee, like Don, lacked sufficient college education. Others simply hadn't measured up to the stiff physical requirements of the US services. Others who were physically fit in every other way, lacked the required 20-20 vision that the American military insisted on for its future aviators. The British, however, with pressure for more and more pilots mounting on the RAF every day, could not afford the luxury of the US qualification criteria. They were accepting otherwise-qualified candidates with 20-40 vision correctable with goggle lenses to 20-20, as well as many whose age, marital status, or even flying ability had ruled them out of the US air arms.

Don was excited by the possibility of entering the RCAF and eventually becoming a member of the Eagles. He tried again and again to persuade his father to sign the papers permitting him to enlist with the Canadians, but to no avail. His father was adamantly opposed, but eventually relented to the extent of agreeing that, if Don finished high school, he would give his permission for him to pursue his dream.

With that all-important high school diploma hanging in the balance, Don devoted himself to his senior studies and performed exceptionally well. During this period he worried about having just forty hours of flight time in his logbook. He knew that the RCAF and RAF required considerably more time than that. In the end, he decided that nothing was more important than becoming a fighter pilot and making his country proud of his war record. He padded his logbook to reflect the required amount of flying time and applied through the Clayton Knight Committee to enlist. In August 1941 he received a reply requesting that he go to the recruiting office in Windsor, Canada, to complete the initial paperwork. That accomplished, he was then sent to the Polaris Flight Academy in Glendale, California, for three months of advanced flying training, followed by two further weeks of intensive training at Ottawa, Canada.

On 11 November 1941, Don was commissioned as a pilot officer in the RAF. A short leave followed and an emotional and tearful farewell as he left Ohio by train for Halifax, Nova Scotia, where he would sail for England. In their parting, Don's father said to him: 'Son, you're on your own now. If you're in trouble just write to me and I'll help you. Whatever it is and wherever you are, I'll help.' Don thanked him and said he would remember that.

CHAPTER TWO

To England

Don Gentile and thirty-seven other Eagle Squadron recruits arrived at Liverpool aboard the tanker *Leticia* in December 1941. Britain had been at war for more than two years. Shortages and hard-ships were a way of life, adding to the adjustment the new Eagles would have to make.

Don was ordered to No. 9 Service Flying Training School at Hullavington, Wiltshire, where he was exposed to flying the RAF way. He flew the Miles Master low-wing monoplane there and greatly enjoyed it. It was a step up from the aircraft he had trained on in Canada; the Master had 700 horsepower and a 225 mph top speed. He began to learn about formation flying and the nerve-wracking business of night flying in England, where the weather, wartime blackouts and barrage balloons made it all the more hazardous. At the end of February 1942, he was posted to No. 57 OTU based at Eshott near Morpeth, Northumberland, where he was introduced to the Vickers-Armstrong Supermarine Spitfire, Britain's legendary fighter plane of the Second World War.

JJ, Bob Richards and Johnny Godfrey shared a cabin on the liner *Queen Elizabeth*, which had been converted to a troop ship for the duration of the war. During a three-day delay before the ship's departure from Halifax, JJ had married his childhood sweetheart and she had accompanied him to the Canadian port. Sailing from Halifax, the ship reached Greenock, Scotland, after a six-day crossing in early November 1942. From Greenock, they travelled by train down to Bournemouth, on the south coast of England, and were billeted at one of the many hotels then being used by the RAF as barracks. At Bournemouth, the three RCAF sergeant pilots had their first fleeting look at the enemy, a lone Focke-Wulf Fw 190, banking low over the city's rooftops on its return to France after dropping its single bomb.

For the next two weeks the three pilots led a life of ease at the seaside, with no official duties, no roll calls, no classes and no one present in authority over them. While JJ pined for his new bride, Johnny and Bob capitalised on a prudent purchase they each had made in Halifax – a dozen pairs of nylon stockings, items that were unobtainable in wartime Britain. They judiciously doled them out to the Bournemouth girls that they met and dated, having what Johnny described as 'a wonderful time'.

On 18 November, the three men were posted to an Advanced Flight Training School at an airfield near the town of Watton, twenty-five miles from Norwich. They settled in at the Watton base and began adjusting to the relative discomforts of life in a cold and draughty Nissen hut on a muddy grass airfield with no hard-surface runways. It was quite a come-down after the comparative luxury of their Bournemouth accommodation, but they soon got used to it. At Watton, they, too, were trained on the Miles Master, an aeroplane employed by the RAF to ease the transition of its fledgling fighter pilots from their previous trainers to the front-line Spitfire. Apart from the slight increase in top speed compared with the Harvards they had flown in Canada, the most obvious difference in the two aircraft was the English braking system of the Master. Unlike the brakes of American and Canadian-manufactured planes, which utilised the rudder pedals for wheel braking, the Master employed a hand brake positioned on the control column. That feature, and the appearance and construction of the plane, left a lot to be desired, in Johnny's opinion. He certainly did not share Don's earlier impression of the plane.

In his early training on the Master, Johnny quickly discovered that the patchwork quilt appearance of the Norfolk countryside around Watton could be extremely confusing. Locating the airfield could be quite a challenge, even with his exceptional eyesight.

Johnny recalled that during this phase of his training:

Our evenings were spent carousing, which for some unexplainable reason kept increasing in tempo. Looking back at this now, I believe that we had psychologically been thrown into a way of life that our young minds were unable to grasp. England had been at war for three years, during which time they had been harassed continually by the enemy. They had withstood this, but a more serious threat was now thrust upon them. The tempo of living had increased, and for some people, morals were the first thing to fall by the wayside. Younger persons of both sexes were rebelling in the only way they knew how.

On Christmas Eve Bob, John and JJ were posted to the same OTU, No. 57 at Eshott, where Don Gentile had undergone final phase training six months earlier. Eager to be off to the OTU and get closer to a combat assignment, they were disappointed to find that it would be a further three days before their transportation to Eshott could be arranged. With the extra time on their hands, they requested forty-eight hour passes to go on leave, but the requests were denied. As it was the Christmas holidays, the boys were somewhat downcast. Bob and JJ decided to go to a party and dance being staged that evening at the sergeants' mess, while Johnny and two other pilots had other plans. They had been invited by an RAF sergeant friend to spend Christmas Day at the home of the sergeant's parents.

After talking it over, they elected to go AWOL (absent without leave) to take advantage of the kind invitation. They thoroughly enjoyed their Christmas Day and the roast goose dinner at the home of their host and returned to base Christmas evening. When they arrived at their Nissen hut, JJ informed them that they had missed an unscheduled roll call at eleven that morning and had been officially posted as AWOL.

The following day, the three men were marched to the office of their CO. They stood to attention as he told them that they would receive disciplinary action within a few days, that they were confined to their quarters and, most disturbing of all, their postings to the OTU were cancelled. The next day they watched as their hut mates packed their duffel bags and departed for the OTU, leaving them to speculate about what sort of additional punishment awaited them. They knew that the RAF maintained a facility at Brighton where punishment was meted out to aircrew deemed guilty of various offences. The rumour mill had it that those sent to Brighton spent their days marching from six in the morning to six in the evening and that the food was abominable.

When they had sweated their fate for two days, they were individually summoned back to the CO's office. Again at rigid attention, Johnny listened as his CO addressed him.

I've heard of a lot of crazy things, Godfrey, but this tops them all. I have two papers on my desk. One is orders made out in your name for you to report to Brighton to undergo a refresher course in military courtesy. The other is your commission, dated August 9th, 1942, stating that you are a Pilot Officer. Since it appears that you were an officer when you took your brief vacation from my command, I cannot take disciplinary action unless I conduct a special court. In other words, you have buggered things up so much that it would take a week of paper work to straighten this mess out. I would consider it a personal favour if you would get the hell off my base.

Of the forty Moncton graduates, five received commissions as pilot officers and Johnny was one of them. The CO wished him good luck and dismissed him. The next day, with orders in hand, Johnny departed for London, where he purchased his officer's uniforms. They were altered and ready for him before the departure time of his train to the OTU that afternoon.

The life of an RAF officer suited Johnny Godfrey very well. He was efficiently looked after by Frankie, the enlisted man appointed as his batman – an aid who saw that his uniforms were always properly maintained and that he awoke to a civilised cup of tea each morning. A batman attended to many little tasks, enabling the pilot officer to concern himself entirely with his own demanding duties. The ambience and refinement of the officers' mess provided a settling influence on Johnny, as did the presence of his fellow officers there, many of them seasoned Battle of Britain veterans.

At Eshott, both Don Gentile and Johnny Godfrey had become acquainted with the Spitfire. Johnny likened the aeroplane to a beautiful woman who, when properly caressed, responded perfectly. Don saw the lovely streamlined machine as the plane he had always longed for and had been born to fly. On the day of his first flight in the Spitfire, Johnny's instructor patiently spent thirty minutes on the wing of the aeroplane explaining the controls and instrumentation. At the end of the lecture, he asked Johnny if he thought he could fly it. 'I believe so,' replied Johnny, and the instructor told him to take it up. Johnny started the big Merlin engine and began taxiing out towards the runway, zigzagging in the way required owing to the restricted forward vision caused by the long, high nose of the plane. Contacting the Eshott tower, he received take-off clearance and turned the aircraft to align it on the centreline of the runway. Gently advancing the throttle, he was amazed at the power unleashed as the little fighter leapt forward. Almost before he realised it, the Spitfire was climbing rapidly away from the runway and Johnny was awkwardly attempting undercarriage retraction, throttle, pitch and trim adjustments in quick succession, trying to 'catch up' with the beautiful machine.

When he reached sufficient altitude, he carefully entered a few gentle turns, a climb and a descent. He was thrilled by the wonderfully quick, subtle responsiveness, the lightness of the controls and the sheer joy of flying this truly exceptional aeroplane. Then another Spitfire appeared alongside, seemingly from out of nowhere. JJ was grinning broadly from the cockpit and Johnny motioned for him to take the lead. He followed JJ through a series of tight turns. At least, to Johnny they seemed tight, as he had yet to develop full confidence in the aeroplane and his ability to handle it in such situations. He waggled his wings, calling off the tail-chase, and departed for the base, accomplishing a reasonably good landing for a first one in a Spitfire.

Tommy Wheler, another friend of Johnny's who was on the same Spitfire course at Eshott recalled:

Johnny was a dashing young pilot. Weren't we all (so we thought)! He and I went up on a dogfight one day in 1943. We squared off at 20,000 feet. I got on his tail and he did a rollover and pulled through. I was about 400–500 yards behind him and trying to close. We were both diving flat out when Johnny's canopy came off and hurtled past me. Johnny pulled out, slowed right down and returned to base. On landing, I had to confirm the incident and there was no problem at all. Johnny was a fine young man and an excellent pilot.

The Spitfire would evolve through twenty-four marks of development. It was one of the best all-round fighters in the world. It was designed by Supermarine's Reginald J. Mitchell, and derived in part from the S-series of racing seaplanes he had designed for Supermarine in the 1920s. K5054, the Spitfire prototype, had first flown from Eastleigh near Southampton in March 1936. It was clear from the start that the little fighter with the big Rolls-Royce Merlin engine handled superbly in the air; it was a fighter pilot's dream come true. It has been described by one aircraft authority as 'the best conventional defence fighter of the war'.

The first RAF unit to receive and operate Spitfire Mk Is was No. 19 Squadron at Duxford in 1938. Production of the plane at that time was extremely limited, but plans were then being formulated to build Spitfires much faster and in enormous quantities at a huge 'shadow factory' to be constructed by the Nuffield Organisation at Castle Bromwich near Birmingham. Sadly, 42-year-old Reginald J. Mitchell died of cancer in June 1937, before his wonderful plane had earned the fame and admiration that was to come.

The Mk I Spitfire was powered by a V-12 Rolls-Royce Merlin II piston engine of 1,030 horsepower. It was capable of a 355 mph maximum speed at a fighting altitude of 19,000 feet and had a service ceiling of 34,000 feet. Its range was just 495 miles, but, as a primarily defensive fighter, it was intended to operate mainly over England and the Channel, giving it a relatively reasonable time aloft in that role. The armament consisted of eight .303 Browning machine-guns, less potent than that of its principal opponent, the Messerschmitt Bf 109E, which mounted two 20 mm cannon and two 7.9 mm machine-guns.

The partner of the Spitfire through the crucial Battle of Britain period in the summer and autumn of 1940 was the Hawker Hurricane. It was a less lovely, slightly slower and less agile fighter than the Spit. However, in the Battle of Britain, more than two-thirds of the fighters available to the RAF were Hurricanes and, while the Spitfire of the day was 30 mph faster than the hump-backed Hurricane, the latter had a superior range of 600 miles. This enabled it to remain in the air longer than either the Spitfire or the Messerschmitt. During that long hot summer, the RAF employed its Hurricanes mainly against vulnerable enemy bombers, while assigning the Spitfires to deal with the German fighters. In the end, the Hurricanes had shot down more planes than any other aircraft type utilised in that campaign. The members of the Eagle Squadrons flew both Hurricanes and Spitfires.

After a period on attachment to No. 65 Squadron, RAF, in order to learn about the Spitfire through actual air fighting experience, Spitfire Chief Test Pilot Jeffrey Quill commented:

We needed more performance, more fuel, and heavier fire-power. I put all these points into a report to Joe Smith [the able successor to R.J. Mitchell at Supermarine] and I made a strong plea for pressing on with the cannon armament. We needed better hitting power and the sooner cannons could be made to work and be introduced into regular service the better.

I also emphasised that, despite anything that pre-war doctrines may have postulated, the Spitfire was primarily an air combat fighter and also, again contrary to a widely held pre-war belief, the day of the dogfight was not over – it would continue to remain with us for the foreseeable future. Therefore the Spitfire should always be considered with this fact firmly in mind.

The Spitfire's ability to out-perform, outfly and preferably outgun enemy fighters in all circumstances was now, in my view, paramount. Some sacrifice of other qualities in the aeroplane would be acceptable if it were necessary in order to achieve these aims.

The Spitfire was very much a pilot's aeroplane. It had an indefinable quality of excitement about it – an unmistakable charisma – which greatly appealed to young and eager pilots, added to which it was the fastest and highest performance fighter of its day and most pilots wanted to fly the best.

At the OTU, Don, Johnny and the others were fully briefed on the enemy they would face in the skies over Nazi-occupied Europe. They were instructed on the nature and quality of the training their adversaries received, the air-fighting experience of the *Luftwaffe* pilots, the tactics they tended to employ and the characteristics of the principal enemy aircraft they would be engaging. They were taught the latest techniques and philosophies of air fighting the RAF way and given the best possible classroom understanding of dogfighting dos and don'ts. These were summed up in the RAF's famous ten rules of air fighting as handed down by one of its finest Battle of Britain combat leaders, Adolf 'Sailor' Malan:

1. Never fly straight and level for more than thirty seconds in a combat area.
2. Always keep a sharp lookout for enemy fighters. Keep your finger out and your head on a swivel. Watch for the enemy in the sun.
3. Height gives you the initiative. Don't waste it.
4. Always turn and face the attacking enemy.
5. Make your decision promptly. It is better to act quickly even though your tactics are not the best.
6. When diving to attack, always leave a portion of your formation above to act as top cover.
7. Wait until you see the whites of your enemy's eyes. Fire short bursts of one or two seconds, and only when your gun sight is definitely on the target.
8. While shooting, think of nothing else. Brace the whole of your body, have both hands on the control stick, concentrate on your gun sight and the target.
9. Go in quickly, punch hard, and get out.
10. Initiative, aggression, air discipline, and teamwork are words that mean something in air fighting.

The OTU intelligence officer informed them:

We will teach you how to fight an air battle. That is your business and you must know it well. But this knowledge is worthless unless you act decisively, instinctively, and fast. We will teach you all the ramifications of the Spitfire and its armament. When the course is completed, you will be able to go find the beggars and clobber them out of the sky.

Along with air and ground gunnery instruction, they were taught ways of improving their flying skills and radio-telephone communicating technique.

In June 1942, Don Gentile completed the OTU course with an assessment of above average as a pilot and average in gunnery. Then came the posting assignments for the graduates of his course. Don was surprised and disheartened when he learned that he had been posted to a flight training school as an instructor.

When I first reached England early in 1942 there was some notion of putting me to work in the Royal Air Force as an instructor, but I took a Spitfire out one day and beat up a greyhound race track, where there was a race going on and the notion ended right there.

When I flew over the dog-track the dogs were tearing after the rabbit and the customers were cheering them on. But when I finished buzzing the track the dogs were running and yowling all over the park and the customers were sprinting after them. Some of the customers, I was told later, even overtook and passed the dogs. Only the mechanical rabbit continued, undaunted, on its way.

Another former Spitfire pilot, Douglas 'Duke' Warren, a Canadian, recalled meeting Don at RAF Hawarden:

I arrived at Hawarden in the evening of April 28th 1942. Here I was to train on Spitfire aircraft and I was excited at the prospect. The next morning I went to the Adjutant's office to sign in. As I turned to leave, the Adj said, 'One of your people has been charged with low flying and is awaiting court martial. He is confined to his quarters and no one goes near him. Would you mind just looking in on him occasionally?' I agreed to do so. Again, I turned to leave and the Adj said, 'Well, really, he is not one of yours, he is an American, but you are all alike and from the same side of the Atlantic.'

I found that Gentile and I were in the same barracks. When I finished unpacking and had a bath I went to his room. His situation was called CB, confined to barracks. I introduced myself, told him I was on the next course, and that I understood he was CB. Don laughed and told me he had beat up the local dog track. He claimed that the dogs had run the wrong way and a Group Captain had lost his bet. This sounded like 'line-shooting' to me, but I thought it might be true. I was rather surprised that he was taking his situation so light-heartedly, as I would have been very concerned if I had been awaiting court martial. I stayed about thirty minutes and then excused myself saying that I had to get to the mess for my meal. He was not allowed in the mess, or out of his room, and his meals had to be brought to him.

I visited Don frequently in the few days before my course started and he was also visited by his defending officer, whom I never met. Don told me he had had some flying experience before joining the

RAF and had wanted to join the US Army Air Corps, but was not accepted due to his limited education at that point. And he told me of the aircraft he had flown. Visiting him was entertaining. He had great stories about cars and parties, girls he had known, and escapades of some of his male friends. It was obvious that Don had not grown up on a farm like my brother and I had. What impressed me was that, at no time did he seem to think he was really in trouble.

I wondered if he ever took anything seriously. Throughout our training, the instructors emphasised that flying was a serious business and discipline was important. I thought Don was seriously lacking in that department, but I couldn't help liking him. After the course started, I looked forward to my visits with him at the end of each day.

Don had a way of talking to the WAAF batwomen that they seemed to enjoy, half teasing, sometimes asking about their families, sometimes tormenting them about their boyfriends, often making remarks that could be interpreted in two different ways, but never crude or rude. They all seemed to like him, though I never saw any indication that these were anything other than casual friendships. I was nineteen at the time and these WAAF girls were, I judged, all quite young, but older than myself. They used to put wildflowers in my room, which no girl in Canada had done.

When the day of Don's court martial finally came, I had to go flying, but I thought about him a good deal that day. Because of the light way he treated the charge against him, and the court martial, I believe I was more worried for him than he was for himself. On landing, I rushed over to his room to learn the bad news. But it was good news. I was astonished! Don was in 'seventh heaven' and talking about flying the next day. On reflection, and knowing how keen he was to fly, I wonder what he would have done had he been found guilty and removed from flying? He told me the details of the court martial. The charge was read, Don's defending officer took his place, and the prosecution started giving the evidence. A technical corporal testified that he had helped P/O Gentile strap into a certain Spitfire and helped him out of the aircraft when he returned. People who were present at the dog track that day said that a Spitfire with certain letters on it flew very low back and forth over the track. The evidence of the corporal proved that Gentile was the pilot in question. Case proved. Gentile was guilty. And then the defending officer got up to speak. He had with him a British Ordnance Survey map dated a certain date. Would anyone like to check this map for authenticity? No one would. He pinned the map on the wall and then measured the distance between the airfield and the dog track.

It was less than three miles. Would anyone like to measure this distance themselves? No one would. He then produced a book called *King's Rules and Regulations Air*, the Bible of the RAF. It contained a definition of low-flying, and it also contained a definition which basically stated that if an aircraft was within a certain distance from an airport, it could not be charged with low-flying because it has to fly low while landing or taking off. The dog track was within that distance from the airport so P/O Gentile could not be charged with low flying . . . a technicality, but it got him off. The charge should have read 'flying an aircraft in a dangerous manner' or something like that. Don was on top of the world. I was amazed. I vowed that if I was ever in trouble, I wanted that defending officer.

Don was reinstated on the course. My course was nearing its end and we were both very busy. We still met each day after flying, but the visits were not as long. We were both being 'pushed' in our flying and, even as young as we were, we both felt tired. A few days after Don had started flying again, I was stunned when I visited him and he told me that he had been low flying again. Hugely pleased with himself, he told how he had flown so low over Rhyl, that his prop wash had thrown sand over the people on the beach there. I didn't doubt his story. I still liked him, but thought he was crazy to do such a thing again.

On completing the course, Don was posted to a new unit, No. 133 (Eagle) Squadron, under the command of Don Blakeslee. With No. 133 (Eagle) Squadron Don flew a Spitfire named *Buckeye Don*, named after his home state of Ohio, the Buckeye state.

In February 1943 Johnny Godfrey returned to his OTU base after a routine formation flying hop. He was met by his instructor, who commended him on his exceptional eyesight and his obvious ability to make the most of the gift. It was the first time Johnny had been truly aware of this special faculty and he was encouraged by the instructor to practise diligently and refine his ability to see the enemy early, before anyone else did, and, crucially, before that enemy spotted him.

On 7 March, Johnny was practising dogfighting with another pilot. After the exercise he was feeling pleased with the results his manoeuvres had achieved. He set the Spitfire up for landing and made a normal approach to the field. Just as his plane was about to touch down, a strong crosswind caught him and pulled the aircraft up. It threatened a dangerous stall. He struggled to regain control, knowing that he should continue flying and make another circuit of the field before making a second landing attempt. Somehow, he felt committed to completing the first attempt and on touching down again, tried to slow the Spitfire with its brakes. At that moment his braking system failed and the machine roared on down the length of the runway. It rolled off into soft mud. Johnny cut the ignition, but the wheels dug into the mud, causing the tail to come up as the Spit went over onto its nose. For a few seconds, he thought the aeroplane would go through the vertical and over onto its back, possibly pinning him in the cockpit. But when the plane reached the vertical, it wobbled and fell back slightly, to balance precariously on its main landing gear.

Johnny found himself hanging in his Sutton harness, as he waited for help from ground personnel. As the ambulance and fire engine skidded to a halt by the aircraft, he was disgusted with himself for having damaged the lovely little fighter, the first aircraft he had damaged since he had begun flying. Once on the ground again, he began to feel considerable pain in his right leg. Checking it, he found no bruise or cut and assumed the injury was of no consequence. However, his right knee was stiff and swollen by the next morning. He reported to the base medical officer, who had the leg x-rayed. The jarring he had received in the Spitfire heavy landing the previous day had aggravated a football injury Johnny had sustained while in high school, and he would have to spend the next few weeks in the base hospital, while Bob and JJ completed their course.

Soon, Johnny too had completed the OTU course and he, Bob and JJ were considered qualified RAF fighter pilots. They had always hoped and expected to transfer eventually to the United States Army Air Force (USAAF) and now that they were fully qualified, they decided to make the move. Their applications for the transfer were approved and Johnny departed from his final RAF posting with ratings of above average as a pilot and excellent in air gunnery.

CHAPTER THREE

At Ease

Audley End station is the closest rail stop to Debden and it was from there that personnel of the Fourth Fighter Group caught a train for London and the occasional forty-eight hour leave. When off duty, American officers and enlisted men could relax in their respective on-base facilities, the officers' mess and the Red Cross Aeroclub. There, they could read, play cards and have a beer. If he was lucky, an American airman would be befriended by a local family and be welcomed by them and fed as one of their own. It was a unique experience for both guest and host. With few exceptions, these boys had never before been outside their own country, some never having crossed the borders of their home state. Equally, many of their English hosts had never before met an American.

For the high-flying, hard-living fighter pilot, the infrequent forty-eight hour pass was hotly anticipated. It meant a brief and welcome time out of war and often a trip to London, where the action was. One airman recalled:

> . . . it was April. You left your overcoat in the belly-tank crate that served as your locker, stuffed some shaving articles in your musette bag and hopped on the 9 or 11 o'clock bus from the main gate. You were taking off for London on a 48. It was spring and you felt eager. Forty-eights to London were a little different each time you went. You remember some of the sights and sounds, and the flat English countryside divided by trees, hedges and waterways. You will never forget the voice of the girl calling trains at Cambridge and the shafts of light cutting through the steam in Liverpool Street Station.

In London the attractions were much the same for the serviceman as for any tourist – the Thames, the Houses of Parliament, St Paul's and Buckingham Palace – all featured on the places to go/things to do list for the American aviator. Off the list, nightclubs were popular – the Nuthouse, the Washington, and the American Melody Club were among the favourites. The American Eagle Club at 28 Charing Cross Road was a regular haunt of US pilots. They often visited Rainbow Corner, the Red Cross-run club in Shaftesbury Avenue. Other attractions included the Windmill Theatre (We Never Closed) and the 'Piccadilly Lilies', who plied their trade by day and night, targeting the well-paid American flyers with precision.

The American officer in London could take his meals at an exclusive eating house known as Willow Run. Located in the Grosvenor House Hotel, Willow Run provided the Yank with food that would make him feel at home, rather than the stodgy, indifferent and meagre meals available in the English restaurants. Pork chops, mashed potatoes, ice cream, sweetcorn, pancakes, fried chicken and steak were offered – luxuries to help the Americans forget the frugality of wartime Britain. Employing chefs whose culinary careers had been interrupted by the draft (from some of America's most interesting restaurants), the Willow Run served delights from the menus of Boston's Kenmore, the El Paso Hilton and Rand's Bakehouse of Morgantown, West Virginia.

The following is an extract from the diary of 1st Lt Jack Raphael, 336th Fighter Squadron Fourth Fighter Group:

11 January 1944 – Millie and I were spotters for a show to Diepholz. Airborne for 3 hours and 20 minutes and got plenty tired. Were vectored out to a 'Mayday' but couldn't make contact. Millie's R/T [radio-telegraphy] was U/S [unserviceable], so I had to transmit and receive for both of us. The group returned to base without making rendezvous and the bombers took a hell of a beating. Lousy weather, solid cloud from 14,000 to 30,000. Millie and I landed in a rainstorm. Caught the late train to London and got a room at the Jules Club. Went to Chez Marcelle for a while and then walked back to the club.

Later that month Raphael wrote in his diary:

21 January 1944 – Show on during the afternoon to Pas de Calais area. On leave so I couldn't go. Richards got an Fw 190. Went to London with Doug Hobert. Stayed at the Reindeer Club. Went to Marcelle's and then to Ling Nam for a Chinese dinner, completely eaten with chopsticks. Had two big raids on the city, 90 Jerry bombers. Ten were shot down. Saw one go down in flames. Noisiest raids I'd heard in a long time. Shrapnel was falling all over the street and killed and injured several people.

Grover Hall, the public relations officer of the Fourth Fighter Group, recalled:

In Piccadilly Circus, about Rainbow Corner, you couldn't see even the big 'Bovril' sign for the American olive drab. They walked about with the girls of many nationalities on their arms. White-helmeted MPs – a source of ceaseless delight and fascination to Englishmen – stood in the entrances to the Underground, which blew its dank breath into the street, and lay in wait for GIs with unbuttoned blouses or one more mild and bitter than they could carry. Through the incredibly congested Circus the lavender-and-old-lace cabs would rage, packed with Americans. You could tell the new arrivals because they rode in clusters of five to eight with the top down, waving a bottle of Scotch and causing the Limeys to remark, 'See? The Americans are the reason spirits are in short supply,'

Night would fall and Piccadilly would assume the shape which will always be a flashing memory with those who did time in the ETO [European Theatre of Operations]. The blackout was rigid, or at least it would have been had it not been for thousands of GIs hurrying about with their torches (Limey for flashlight). You could tell an American from any other in the dark because their flashlights were larger and more powerful. From lower Regent Street, they made Piccadilly look like a jar of fireflies in a closet. At first blackout the celebrated 'Piccadilly Commandos' would begin walking the night, as much a part of the scene as the doorman in front of the Regent Palace Hotel. Inappropriately, the famous statue of Eros, God of Love, was crated during the war. They were more an institution than a facility, and few GIs (I speak for Debden), permitted themselves a conclusive encounter. They were as alert as a bell captain and aggressive, approaching everything in olive drab with a parroted American slang greeting, which was ridiculous when conveyed in a British accent. Their honorariums were enormous (and downright incredible when they walked under a light). But they were an integral part of Piccadilly's teeming pageantry.

Soon the soldier began to feel at home, the first sign being that he spent two days in London without gawking at the barrage balloons loafing over the city. He got caught in air raids and learned to tell the big ones from the little ones by the whistle. He became allergic to exposed lights and blacked them out with reflex action. He began counting British currency as easily as US. There was just one thing whose hatefulness never diminished, the weather. Every day he felt as though his skin had accumulated another layer of mould.

Personnel of the 4th Group variously bled and sweated for two and a half years to prove itself the worst enemy the Germans had among American fighter groups. Generally they relieved the pace with boozing, roistering and giving the girls a break.

Consider a party night on pay day.

In the late afternoon the public address system in the Officers' Club would reverberate with a clarion call: 'There will be a small crap game in the game room.' You would see them bounce up and soon, perhaps $1,500 in sweaty pound notes would be swapping hands.

The approximately 250 officers at Debden bought 700 bottles of throat-scratching whiskey a month (at 75 shillings per black-market bottle, that came to $10,500). The Colonel got what few bottles there were of pre-war Haig's Pinch Bottle; majors got the wartime Pinch Bottle; the rest of us got Dennison's.

Girl guests at the dances began arriving at 6 o'clock, from London to Land's End, some on bicycles. They had to sign name and addresses at the guard post at the gate for reasons of military security (this appeared a less pointless precaution later when we learned about German intelligence operations at Debden). They would go into the dining room with their dates for dinner. The girl waitresses tried not to stare at the girls, but having served the officers daily they took a possessive interest in appraising their tastes. Others had a more basic interest. Naturally they were generally disapproving and were not always inarticulate about it.

The enlisted men would likewise be having a party at the Red Cross Aero Club. From miles about groups of girls, most of them British WACs, were fetched in truck convoys. The men were not allowed to take the girls out of the building for walks and talks, one reason being that the Colonel was responsible for getting them back to their stations by midnight. So everything outside the building was off-limits, and especially the air-raid shelters. But love, and its reasonable facsimiles, find a way and the favorite escape exit was a window in the girls' room. There was an unending stream of traffic through this lavatory window, which often brought squeals from girls who had not repaired to the water closet for the purposes of egress.

The drawing power of Debden balls could best be seen by the visiting aircraft parked about the control tower. There were P-47s, Lightnings, Mustangs, Marauders, Forts, Libs, Tiger Moths, Lancasters, Typhoons. Even the Navy was represented – PBY Catalinas. Café society of the ETO was assembled.

The tone of Debden parties had been handed down by the RAF, whose pilots first occupied the Officers' Mess. Just before the RAF turned the base over to the Americans, an RAF fighter pilot rode down the 150 yard corridor through the building on a motorcycle. The RAF's American successors had no intention of letting Debden's old traditions perish or even languish. On many nights, with a tough show coming up at dawn, everyone would go to a movie, grab a buffet snack, write the folks and go quietly to bed. But other times, especially when weather kept the pilots grounded, you might hear one emptying a clip of .45 caliber slugs into the walls of his room. A pilot whose nerves were on edge with too much combat might be seen to empty his pistol at a Roscoe Machine [a one-armed bandit] that refused to pay off. There were two roommates who sometimes lay on their backs in bed and shot the lights out as the pistol was closer than the light switch.

Most of the parties were conventionally shrill, jitter-buggy and raucous, but undistinguished. On unpredictable occasions, however, over-wrought pilots would embark on a binge calculated to take the place of air battles that the weather was precluding. One particular night several of the pilots left the party to commandeer an ambulance, which they filled with flares and smoke pots. All around the perimeter of the flying field they sped in the ambulance. The officer-of-the-day charged after them in a jeep. The back door of the ambulance came open like a bomb bay and the pilots began firing Very gun flares at the pursuing law. The ambulance was the only vehicle on the station without a governor and it pulled away from the OD's jeep like a rum-runner from a revenue agent.

Every once in a while American airmen were sent off to a Red Cross facility in the countryside for a week of rest and relaxation. Several large country houses had been turned over to the USAAF for use as 'rest homes'. The Air Force recognised the importance of such interludes in restoring war-weary flyers to combat-ready condition. Coombe House, at Shaftesbury, was a rest home run by American Red Cross girls. One of them, Ann Newdick, wrote of her life at Coombe House – 'the flak farm', as US airmen called it.

It's January, so the morning sun is rare and welcome. Breakfast is bacon and eggs. Apparently the grapevine knew it too because half the house is up for breakfast, twenty or so combat fliers disguised in sweaters, slacks and sneakers. Plans are afoot for golf, tennis and shooting skeet in the back yard, but the loudest conversation and most uproarious kidding centres around the four who are going to ride to the hounds in a country fox hunt. On a rainy day there's almost as much activity at Coombe House – the badminton court in the ballroom is our chief pride. But nevertheless, the Army calls it a Rest Home. It looks as English as the setting for a Noël Coward play, but even as you approach the house you discover that actors and plot are American. You meet a girl in scuffed saddle shoes and baggy sweater bicycling along a shaded drive with a dozen young men. You'd guess it was a co-ed's dream of a college house party – not a military post to which men are assigned and where girls are stationed to do a job. We have so much fun that we usually forget its military purpose, and so much the better, because this house party is a successful experiment to bring combat fliers back to the peak of their efficiency.

There are four of us here, American girls sent overseas by the Red Cross. Never in our wildest dreams did we expect such a job. At first we felt almost guilty to be having such a good time. I was talking about what a picnic it was to one of the boys. 'That's the way it should be,' he said with authority. When I looked again I remembered that he was a medical officer who'd been at Coombe for about six weeks. In our conversation, I found out that he was Captain David Wright, Psychiatric Consultant for the Eighth Air Force. He had spent his six weeks in careful observation to decide the value of Rest Homes. 'Coombe House, and the others like it,' he said, 'represents the best work of preventative medicine in the ETO. Very definitely Rest Homes are saving lives – and badly needed airmen – by returning men to combat as more efficient fliers.' A remarkable percentage of men who finish their tours have had a chance to be in Rest Homes sometime during their combat tour. There isn't any one word to describe the varying states of mind of combat fliers when they are just plain tired. Tired because it's hard work flying a P-47 or navigating a B-17 or shooting out of the waist window of a B-24. Tired as any-one is after intense mental and muscular strain – intermittent though it is – the lulls in between are not long enough for the flier to get past the let-down stage before he plunges into danger again.

At first the Air Force ran these Rest Homes alone. After two had been established, a large part of the responsibility was transferred to the American Red Cross to make them as un-military as possible. Army quartermaster outdoes itself on food, and 'Cooky' in the kitchen does it to perfection. Fried chicken, steaks, eggs and ice cream are regular items on the menu, all served by pretty waitresses. 'Irish Mike' and Cooky, and all the rest of them are contributions of the Red Cross which disguise the technical and military nature of Coombe House almost beyond recognition, and we four American girls show no obvious solicitude for anyone's morale. We turn down an invitation to play bridge if we want to dance with someone else. Lack of Army demands and freedom from regulations help create the free and easy tempo of the place. The whole feeling is one of such warmth and such sincerity that men come away knowing they have shared an experience of real and genuine living.

The building that housed the Prince's Garden Club is long gone. In April 1943 it provided a London billet for up to forty American servicemen during their leaves in London. Johnny Godfrey remembered it:

The taxi stopped in front of a four-storey building sporting the American and Red Cross flags. There was nothing imposing about the building. It resembled all the others that formed a triangle around a carefully tended grass plot. After paying the taxi driver a three-bob fare, I sauntered into the place which for all the time I was to be in England would be my home away from home. There were forty beds available for non-commissioned officers and officers who wished to spend their leave in London.

Johnny met Bob and JJ at the Prince's Garden Club and they introduced him to Mrs Marise Campbell, an American woman in charge of the club. Mrs Campbell, who they were soon to call 'Mrs C' had three sons, all serving in the armed forces and she quickly came to regard the three pilots as 'my boys' too. She had volunteered to serve in the Red Cross when her husband, a surgeon, was called into the Army. Charming and gracious, anyone could see instantly why she had been chosen to direct the club. Kindly, sensitive and generous, this very special woman looked after the boys as though they were her own. They quickly discovered the wisdom of having her look after their money for them when they were in town, doling it out to them like an allowance and, in so doing, saving them from many an indiscretion and insolvency. Crap games were an ever-present danger in wartime London and the restraint provided by Mrs C, at the boys' behest, was in their best interests.

Mrs C owned a dog – a friendly French poodle called Inky. The boys decided they wanted a dog of their own and Mrs C offered to help by telephoning the dog pound to see what they might have available for adoption. The cost of a dog from the pound was ten shillings. Johnny, JJ and Bob looked over the enormous selection at the pound and unanimously chose a little black and white dog of 'undetermined ancestry' with long hair that completely covered his face. They named him Lucky.

Johnny recalled:

Back at the club we were met by Inky, but instead of bounding up to us as he usually did, he seemed to hesitate, and looked questioningly up at the object I held in my arms. Then Lucky took charge of the situation. He jumped from my arms to meet Inky – and with that, Lucky officially joined the club. Lucky and Inky soon became bosom buddies, but it was always such a comical sight to see them together: Inky was a standard-size poodle, and Lucky, who was eight months old, was only about one foot off the ground. It was not too long before we discovered that our new addition was lacking in house manners. All three of us adopted the habit of carrying Kleenex in our hip pockets so that Lucky's little accidents would not be discovered by Mrs C.

The boys' next stop was the 12th Replacement Depot, Stowe, followed two weeks later by a three-month stint at the Combat Crew Replacement Centre, Atcham, near Shrewsbury in Shropshire, a base that had only recently been taken over by the Americans. At Stowe, the boys experienced a concentrated two-week lesson in how to behave as American air force officers. They, together with seventeen other newly commissioned USAAF officers, spent the fortnight receiving a basic grounding in the fine points of American military courtesy and order. That completed, they left for Atcham and their first encounters with the Thunderbolt It was here that Johnny was to surrender his cherished Spitfire for the much larger and rather brutish Republic P-47 Thunderbolt. He commented, 'In contrast to the sleek, small Spitfire, I found the P-47 to be huge and cumbersome. What I enjoyed most in this plane, however, was the roominess in the cockpit'. In his three months at Atcham, Johnny accumulated forty-five hours' flying in the Thunderbolt, learning about air-to-air gunnery and formation flying in the big beast.

While awaiting their permanent USAAF postings, the boys logged relatively little flying time in the new P-47s. The rest was party time. The CO of the base was the sort who loved a good time, excelled in the many crap games, and enjoyed the best liquor to be had and the loveliest girls in the area.

John, Bob and JJ were quartered with nine others in a Nissen hut as there were no officers' quarters available during their stay at the base. The trouble came one drunken Saturday night when JJ decided to spray one of the other pilots, Bob 'Dutch' Wehrman, with the fire extinguisher. Wehrman immediately retaliated by emptying the fire bucket over JJ. Some of the others were caught in the line of fire, departed and quickly returned with a hose. The water fight intensified and soon everyone in the hut was involved, with clothing and beds a mess and a lot of water on the floor. Johnny recalled that poor little innocent Lucky looked like a drowned rat. In the chaos, Johnny was accidentally hit in the forehead by a flying water bucket. Bob and JJ rushed him by jeep to the base hospital where the duty doctor sewed him up with half a dozen stitches. Later, the boys managed to contrive a reasonably dry place to sleep by turning their mattresses over. The next morning the CO dropped by to look over the scene of the crime. True to his nature, instead of applying strict disciplinary action, he allocated a selection of separate rooms for the residents of the flooded Nissen, explaining that he feared they would kill each other if required to continue living in the hut.

CHAPTER FOUR

Debden

From the diary of 1st Lt Jack Raphael, 336th Fighter Squadron:

1 January 1944 – Slept in until noon and really enjoyed it. A release came through until dawn of the 2nd, so no flying was done. Most of the boys were busy recuperating from the party, anyhow. Lots of hangovers and overnight guests in evidence. Church was slightly banged up from passing out on the way home. George and I put in an hour of Link just to start the year out right. Weren't very keen about it, but business is business. After supper Engstrom came over to play cards. After he left, I went to Nelson and Schlegel's room, George brought down the remains of some Christmas packages, and we talked and ate until nearly 01:00 am.

Then came the day when orders arrived, posting Johnny and Bob to the Fourth Fighter Group, which was stationed at Debden, about fifteen miles south-east of Cambridge. JJ was posted to the 356th Fighter Group at Martlesham Heath in Suffolk near Ipswich. The postings marked the first time that the trio had been split up and all three were saddened by it. They all hoped that, somehow, JJ would eventually be able to transfer to the Fourth.

When they arrived at the Debden base, Johnny's first reaction was 'Hot damn, no more grass runways for us. And look at all those beautiful P-47s at the edge of the field.'

The village of Debden and the air base are just a few miles south-east of the town of Saffron Walden in the county of Essex. Today, the base is known as Carver Barracks. It was a pre-Second World War RAF station with permanent buildings, most of which remain in use by the British Army.

The aerodrome came into being in the mid-1930s. The property was then owned by Mr A. C. Kettley, one of a long line of Kettleys who had farmed the land near Debden village as far back as the locals could recall. It was Mr Kettley's plan that he and his descendants would continue to farm that land for many generations to come and this wish looked set to be fulfilled until one early evening in May 1934. The pilot of a new RAF Bristol Bulldog fighter lost power while returning from an exhibition flight at Ipswich. Unable to make it to an airfield, the hapless pilot was forced to put his aircraft down in the nearest farm field of sufficient size, which happened to be that of Mr Kettley. Gliding over the farmer's head, the Bulldog then inscribed a long, deep cut in the tall wheat.

Happy to have survived the experience, the pilot extricated himself from his machine and climbed down to encounter the enraged farmer. 'What are you doing in my wheat field?' An argument ensued, but tempers soon cooled and the aviator invited the countryman to the nearest pub for a glass or two. However, relations between Mr Kettley and the RAF soon became strained again. When Air Ministry crash investigators showed up to look into the incident, they also looked over the Kettley environs. Within days, some RAF officers arrived to tell the farmer: 'Kettley, we've got good news for you. We've come to buy your farm for an aerodrome site.' 'To hell with you,' Kettley responded, but his resistance was short-lived and in vain. The RAF could sense the coming of war and would not be denied.

The Debden base was extremely important to the RAF during the Battle of Britain in the summer and autumn of 1940. Much later, it came under the command of the USAAF with the presence of the Fourth Fighter Group. During the RAF occupancy, Mr Kettley was mollified somewhat and given a pass allowing him to walk the station at will.

Unlike most of the fifteen fighter group stations of the Eighth Air Force, Debden had been built as a permanent RAF station. It had substantial brick barracks that featured steam heat, tennis and squash courts, and a billiards room. As Public Relations Officer Grover Hall recalled:

. . . [there were] napkin rings, flowers, waitresses, civilian orderlies called batmen, and RAF silverware. . . . [a far cry from] the dismal Nissen hut stations, metal tent cities where you slept around a pot-bellied little stove in one county and went to the can in the next county.

The war correspondent William McDermott of *The Cleveland Plain Dealer* shared the same view:

After having taken board and room in several different bomber stations I thought I ought to get around to a fighter base and see how the other half lives . . . A slightly alcoholized bombardier recently spelled out the prevailing sentiment, 'Every time I see a fighter pilot I want to kiss him. A lot of us wouldn't be here if it wasn't for those babies.' There are photographs and drawings of their former officers on the walls, some long dead, some happily alive and thriving. A famous British artist has his studio in one of the mess hall rooms. The first shot in the Battle of Britain was fired from this post . . . I did not expect the additional comforts this station offers . . . you can have your breakfast as late as 8:30 in pleasant contradistinction with the infantry's stoic 7 am, and if you sneak in at 9 o'clock you still have a good chance of being fed. The food is superior to that offered by some de luxe London hotels. It was the first time I had looked an egg in the eye for the several months I have been in England. For the first time on a visit to an air force station I was able to sleep without shivering in the usual sleeping garments.

Like the other fighter stations of the Eighth Air Force, Debden was populated by about 1,500 officers and men. There were females, too – three American Red Cross girls and a number of young waitresses serving meals in the mess. The three squadrons of the group were each composed of a small number of pilots to fly the sixteen planes in each squadron, and about 200 enlisted men who functioned as clerks, cooks, drivers, armourers and mechanics. There was also a service group, comprising three squadrons, to maintain the station facilities and carry out some of the aircraft repairs.

When Bob and Johnny first entered the officers' mess, they noted the large lounge with its fireplace in one corner, the big padded leather chairs, the billiards room, the writing room, card room, bar and the dining room. They saw a number of pilots relaxing in the lounge, reading, talking and drinking. No mission was scheduled that day and they were soon pleased to encounter a few of the boys they had trained with in Canada, from the OTU and Atcham. They learned that they would have to wait their turn before being allocated quarters in the officers' mess. For the time being, they would share room 5 in building number 7, one of the individual houses near the mess.

The sound that greeted them there was the Ink Spots singing 'Paper Doll'. It was the only record owned by their nearby neighbour in number 7, Bert Waterman. He played the tune constantly and Bob and Johnny vowed to take up a collection to buy Waterman some new records.

The popularity of 'Paper Doll' in that period is further attested to by a habit developed by Lieutenant Ray Wild, a B-17 pilot stationed at Podington in Bedfordshire. In the early days of Wild's tour of duty he, and many of the other fliers on the base (who were honest about it) knew the meaning of fear and its effect on the days when they were scheduled to go on missions.

I remember that just before my first raid – the one where you are really frightened to death – I went into the john in the operations tower. Didn't have to go, but just went in and sat on the john. That was when the song 'Paper Doll' had just come out and somebody had written all the words on the wall in there. Well, just through nothing but being nervous, I sat there and memorised those words.

The mission was the 8 October 1943 raid on Frankfurt, and it proved to be a rough one. Wild's plane returned with a two-foot hole in one side, one engine out, three of its six elevator control cables shot in two, and its radio operator seriously wounded. But because the plane did get back and all its crew survived, said Wild, 'From then on I sat in that same john every mission morning. And you know, even to this day I know every word of "Paper Doll"'.

Wild's third raid was the Schweinfurt mission of 14 October 1943, an attack in which sixty Eighth Air Force B-17s were shot down by flak and fighters. Until that day Wild had been keeping a diary of his experiences in the air force. After it, he figured no one would be surviving a full tour and no longer saw any point in maintaining the diary.

Johnny and Bob took a brief tour of the base administrative area on their way to report to the station commander. They took in the Red Cross club for the enlisted men, the base hospital, the armament building, tennis and volley ball courts, the movie house, post exchange, photography shop, the enlisted men's barracks and, finally, the station headquarters building. All the buildings were painted with camouflage colours. The forty-eight Thunderbolts out on the airfield were the focus and entire *raison d'être* of the 1,500 officers and men on the Debden base.

Johnny and Bob produced their orders for the adjutant at the head-quarters and were asked to wait a few minutes until the CO, Colonel Peterson, was available to greet them. Peterson had commanded the original Eagle Squadron and had been flying with the RAF since 1940. He was twenty-three, a full colonel and was credited with downing five German planes. He had earned the British DFC and DSO, as well as the American DFC and DSC decorations. The boys were summoned into

Peterson's office and saluted him briskly. He welcomed them and said he hoped they would carry on in the tradition of the group. He told them what he expected of pilots in his command and finished by saying that No. 336 Squadron was short of two pilots and they were to report to Major 'Spike' Miley and be in his command.

In the spring of 1942, the Eagle Squadrons were well established, with No. 71 Squadron at Debden, No. 121 at North Weald and No. 133 at Biggin Hill. These were the best, most prestigious stations, in the forefront of Fighter Command's offensive. Under the commands of Gus Daymond, Chesley Peterson and Carroll McColpin, the squadrons had become seasoned and fully effective. They were great favourites of the press, and Hollywood showed interest with a motion picture called *Eagle Squadron*. Introduced by the popular war correspondent Quentin Reynolds, the cast included Robert Stack, Diana Barrymore, Jon Hall, Eddie Albert, Nigel Bruce, Lief Erickson, John Loder, and the Eagles themselves. Most of the action was filmed at the bases of the Eagle Squadrons in England, but the filmmakers hadn't appreciated or accounted for the reality of war. Every time a pilot was lost, the script had to be rewritten and previously exposed footage had to be scrapped. In the end, the filmmakers gave up and moved the production back to Hollywood. The resulting movie was a schmaltzy, romanticised disaster. It was too much for the attending Eagles to stomach and most of the pilots walked out of its London premiere, even though the King was present.

The Fourth Fighter Group of the USAAF had been activated on 12 September 1942 at Bushey Hall in Hertfordshire, England. On 22 August 1942, the three American Eagle Squadrons of the RAF were transferred to the USAAF and would constitute the Fourth Fighter Group. The squadrons were based at Debden and a satellite field, Great Sampford, also in Essex.

The first Eagle Squadron, No. 71, had been created at RAF Church Fenton, Yorkshire, on 19 September 1940. Initially, the squadron flew Brewster Buffalo aircraft, but by November they had been re-equipped with Hawker Hurricanes. Combat operations for No. 71 Squadron began on 5 February 1941 at their new base, Kirton-in-Lindsey, Lincolnshire. The second Eagle Squadron, No. 121, was established at Kirton-in-Lindsey on 14 May 1941, its Hurricanes entering combat in July. Finally, No. 133 Eagle Squadron was formed at Coltishall on 29 July 1941 and the men began their operational flying in Supermarine Spitfire IIas from Fowlmere, Cambridgeshire, that October.

In September 1942 Carroll 'Red' McColpin was in command of No. 133 Eagle Squadron, which was then stationed at Biggin Hill, Kent. The Eagle Squadrons were still functioning then as part of the RAF. McColpin recalled:

I knew that a big mission to Morlaix was coming up, but I'd been ordered to transfer to the USAAF. Ordered. I kept delaying it, week after week. We were down at Biggin Hill, but 133 was being moved up to Great Sampford, near Debden. The mission was being laid on . . . then off . . . then on again.

I decided I wouldn't go and leave the outfit until the mission was over with. I was gonna lead that mission. Then, General 'Monk' Hunter called up from Fighter Command headquarters of the Eighth Air Force and said, 'I understand you haven't transferred,' and I said, 'Yes, sir.' He just said, 'Well, you get your butt in there and transfer, right now!' To which I came back, 'Sir, I'm waiting for this Morlaix mission and I'm trying to keep enough boys in here to run it, 'cause it's a big one.' 'To heck with that . . . you get in there and transfer,' Hunter replied. 'Well, sir,' I said, 'you understand that I'm in the Royal Air Force, and I have an ops instruction here which says we are going to Morlaix when they lay it on. I'm the CO here, and I've got my squadron on the line.' With that he snorted and hung up. About an hour later I got a call from an air marshal in the group. 'McColpin, do you take orders from me?' I said, 'I certainly do, sir. Yes, sir.' That's how I came to transfer over.

Twenty-seven-year-old Red McColpin brought a rare maturity to the youthful Eagles. While not doubting that his age and experience contributed to his survival and success, there were other factors that he counts as crucial.

You could still use luck. Every once in a while a part would break or fail on your aeroplane while you were flying, but you could eliminate or reduce your need for luck by making sure your plane was 100 per cent ready to go. Then, as double insurance, you'd always make sure you knew where you were going to land in any emergency.

McColpin's policy was careful planning, and he followed certain personal rules. They included not living it up in the pubs and clubs – all part of maintaining the peak physical condition in which he prided himself. He had first-rate eyesight, good hearing, physical strength . . . and endurance. Flying four hundred fighter missions without once being hit and never losing a pilot when leading his flight proved the wisdom of his philosophy. His success as flight commander led to his promotion to commander of No. 133 Squadron. His men admired and respected his leadership qualities. He was once gratified to overhear one of them say, 'Well . . . I'll go with McColpin any place he'll go.' 'Amen' was the response of the other pilots in the room. But despite this vote of confidence, there was still an occasional voice of dissent, such as when his pilots became aware that pilots in other squadrons were getting promoted more quickly. McColpin told them bluntly that he would transfer them if they wanted out, but they should remember one thing: the other outfits were taking the casualties. Did they want to be live pilot officers or dead flight lieutenants?

The Morlaix raid was a disaster and a sad way for the Eagle Squadrons to bow out of the RAF. A British pilot, Gordon Brettell, was placed in command of No. 133 Squadron, and led the Morlaix mission on 26 September in Red McColpin's place.

The raid required the Eagles to escort American bombers hitting the Brest peninsula, flying out across the widest part of the English Channel, over a heavily defended area, and back again. By 26 September, No. 133 Squadron was at Great Sampford, waiting to be absorbed into the USAAF, but the men would still fly the mission. The unit was sent down to Bolt Head, a forward base located between Dartmouth and Plymouth in Devon. Here, its pilots were to refuel, be briefed for the mission and join the other two squadrons flying it, Nos 401 and 412 (Canadian). On the flight down to Bolt Head, the weather was bad and getting worse, threatening the impending mission.

Without McColpin's discipline, the pilots of No. 133 Squadron were careless in preparing for the Morlaix mission. Most didn't bother to attend the briefing. Only Brettell and one other pilot were briefed for the raid. In the briefing, the Met officer gave a tragically erroneous piece of information – a predicted thirty-five knot headwind at the mission altitude of 28,000 feet. Further, no one knew precisely when the bombers were to take off, or their precise *rendezvous* time with the fighters. The pilots lounged under the wings of their Spitfires and waited. McColpin's key word, 'planning', certainly did not apply. The take-off was a mess. There were near-collisions; pilots didn't receive proper instructions about radio channels; some even left maps and escape kits behind.

Flying with auxiliary fuel tanks, thirty-six Spitfires headed out to meet the bombers. There was no sign of them, and the fighters continued on course and called by radio for news of the bombers. The predicted thirty-five knot headwind had been a major miscalculation. Both bombers and fighters – miles apart – were being whisked along by a 100-knot tail-wind. One of the pilots later commented: 'It all added up to a streaking catastrophe.' Miles ahead of the fighters, the bombers had unknowingly crossed the Bay of Biscay above a blanket of cloud. They discovered their problem when they reached the Pyrenees mountains, and dumped their bombs and swung back to the north on a reciprocal course, meeting the Spitfires head-on. The fighters turned north as well. By this time, all the aircraft had vanished from the radar plots in England, and communications between bombers, fighters and their various bases were a shambles. Having been airborne for two hours and fifteen minutes, the Spitfire pilots believed they were near home again and began to let down through the cloud cover. A coastline appeared, which they assumed to be England. It was, in fact, the French coast, and they passed over Brest harbour and through a massive flak barrage. In moments, ten Spitfires were lost, four pilots killed and six downed and captured, among them the CO, Gordon Brettell. He would later be one of the fifty Allied prisoners-of-war to be executed by the SS for taking part in the Great Escape from Stalag Luft III. Two other Spitfires failed to return to Bolt Head. Morlaix was a most unfortunate final mission for the Eagles.

Don Gentile was assigned to the Morlaix mission as a spare. He would participate in it if any of the other pilots were forced to abort. Luckily for him, there were no aborts. As a member of No. 133 Squadron, Don became what might be called a 'founding member' of the Fourth Fighter Group. On a rain-swept parade ground at Debden, on 29 September, Don listened to the words of RAF Air Chief Marshal Sholto Douglas as he spoke to the assembled former Eagles:

> I would have wished that on this, my first opportunity of addressing all three Eagle Squadrons together on one station, that my words should have been other than words of farewell. We, of Fighter Command, deeply regret this parting, for in the course of the past eighteen months we have seen the stuff of which you are made, and we could not ask for better companions with whom to see this fight through to a finish. But we realise as you too must realise that your present transfer to your own country's air force is in the long run in the best interests of our joint cause. The United States Army Air Force's gain is very much the Royal Air Force's loss.
>
> The losses to the *Luftwaffe* will no doubt continue as before. In the eighteen months which have elapsed since your first unit became fully operational, Eagle pilots have destroyed some seventy-three enemy aircraft – the equivalent of about six squadrons of the *Luftwaffe* – and probably destroyed and damaged a great many more. The actual official total of destroyed is, I believe, seventy-three and one-half,

the half being part of a Dornier shared with a British squadron as a symbol of Anglo-American cooperation. Of the seventy-three and one-half enemy aircraft destroyed, forty-one have been claimed by the senior Eagle Squadron 71 – a record of which they may very well be proud, but one which I understand the other two squadrons are determined will not long remain unchallenged.

It is with great personal regret that I today say goodbye to all you boys whom it has been my privilege to command. You joined us readily of your own free will when our need was greatest and before your country was actually at war with our common enemy. You were the vanguard of that host of your compatriots who are now helping to make these islands a base from which to launch the great offensive we all desire. You have proved yourself fine fighters and good companions and we shall watch your future with confidence.

There are those of your number who are not here today – these sons of the United States who were the first to give their lives for their country. We of the RAF no less than yourselves will always remember them with pride. Like their fathers who fought and died with the American vanguard of the last war, the Lafayette Squadron, so will those Eagles who fell in combat ever remain the honoured dead of two great nations.

And now I have some news for you. The Air Council, anxious to give tangible expression to the gratitude which we all feel for the great work you have done, is going to ask each of you to accept a small personal memento of your services to the Royal Air Force. The memento will take the form of a medallion, and though it has not been possible in the short time available to have this medallion struck and ready by today, it is hoped that its presentation will be made in the very near future.

I hope that these emblems will serve as a pleasant reminder of your comradeship with the Fighter Command of the Royal Air Force, a comradeship which we have been very proud to share and which I, as your Commander-in-Chief, shall always remember with gratitude and affection.

Goodbye and thank you, Eagle Squadron of the Royal Air Force. And good hunting to you, Eagle Squadron of the United States Air Force.

So parted the Eagles and the RAF. It had not always been a comfortable relationship, but it had laid the foundations for Anglo-American cooperation in air fighting, had seen seventy-three enemy air-craft destroyed and had hatched the Fourth Fighter Group of the Eighth

Air Force. The Fourth Fighter Group at Debden became the highest-scoring fighter group in the USAAF. A German propaganda statement referred to them as the 'Debden Gangsters'. The Eagles are still remembered by the British. A returning Eagle veteran was surprised to receive a free taxi ride when revisiting London in recent years. He asked why. The driver's answer was, 'You were an Eagle. You already paid.'

The composition of the new Fourth Fighter Group was as follows: No. 71 Eagle Squadron was reborn as the 334th Fighter Squadron, No. 121 Eagle Squadron became the 335th Fighter Squadron and No. 133 Eagle Squadron was now the 336th Fighter Squadron. The 336th Fighter Squadron would soon be home to both Don Gentile and Johnny Godfrey.

In October, November and December 1942, the Spitfires of the Fourth Fighter Group engaged in relatively little operational flying and several former Eagles were reassigned to other units in the fledgling Eighth Fighter Command. They were soon replaced by other American pilots who had been serving in the RAF, but not in the Eagle Squadrons. What combat flying that did take place consisted mainly of convoy patrols and short-range ground-strafing attacks. Additionally, the pilots were occupied with practice missions and further ground instrument instruction in Link trainers.

While the Fourth Fighter Group was technically the newest American fighter outfit in England, its pilots were, in fact, the most combat-experienced and well-prepared in the European theatre of operations. At their Debden base, there was an undercurrent of protest among the pilots when it was announced that Eighth Fighter Command had decided to convert the Fourth Fighter Group to the new Republic P-47 Thunderbolt. During January 1943, the first of the group's new P-47C Thunderbolts began to arrive at Debden. Concurrently, a number of the group's pilots were temporarily detached to Atcham for training on the P-47. Of the three Fourth Fighter Group squadrons, only the 334th's ground crews had received instruction on the Thunderbolt (at Bovingdon on their arrival in England) and it was to the 334th Fighter Squadron that the first of the new fighters was allocated at Debden. The Spitfires of the 334th Fighter Squadron were donated to the other two Debden squadrons while they awaited their conversion to Thunderbolts.

In his book *P-47 Thunderbolt*, William N. Hess says of the big fighter:

Originally the Republic P-47 was to have been a conventional 1939 design, but only lightly armed with two machine-guns and powered by the new Allison V-1710 liquid-cooled engine, the lightweight aircraft would have been miserably obsolete before the prototype was finished.

Alexander Kartveli, the brilliant chief engineer of Republic, disagreed with the programme, and once war had erupted in Europe, he eagerly sought performance information from the combat area. Under his leadership, Republic completely redesigned its aircraft and produced one of the outstanding fighters of the Second World War. The new XP-47B was a heavyweight built around the Pratt & Whitney R-2800 engine, which developed 2,000 horsepower. A turbo-supercharger made it a high-altitude performer and the light armament was replaced by four .50 machine-guns in each wing.

The heavy fighter was not an instant winner with the pilots that initially took it to combat. The American ex-Eagle Squadron pilots hated it from the beginning, but the 56th Fighter Group pilots who initially trained on the P-47 loved it. Low-altitude air-to-air combat remained a problem until a paddle blade propeller was added, but high-altitude combat was a different story.

Its short range was a distinct handicap until the auxiliary fuel tank problems had been resolved, but when it came to strafing and dive-bombing the big P-47 excelled. Following D-Day in France, the Thunderbolts performed magnificently in ground support until the end of the war.

A late arrival in the Far East and the Pacific, the P-47 did a fine job in the ground support role in Burma and China. In the South and Central Pacific it served in small numbers until late in the war, but wherever it served it turned in a brilliant performance, marked by the great destruction of which it was capable. Despite its great capability, however, the P-47 was soon scrapped after the war. Who was to know that as early as 1950 its ground-support performance would have been a real blessing in Korea.

When that first Thunderbolt arrived in England at the end of December 1942, it was turned over to the technical section of the Eighth Fighter Command for evaluation. Testing began immediately to determine the positive and negative characteristics of the new aircraft. In two weeks of evaluation, the P-47 was run through mock dogfights with the Fw 190. It was shown that the German fighter could readily outrun and out-turn the big Republic fighter at altitudes up to 15,000 feet. Importantly, however, the test series found that the Thunderbolt was superior in performance at altitudes above 15,000 feet, where it could easily out-turn and outrun the German plane. The test results did little to allay the concerns of the Debden pilots, but did, at least, add to their knowledge of the new plane.

The pilots of the Fourth Fighter Group continued to fly defensive and convoy patrols in their Spitfires into January 1943. Meanwhile, a new fighter group arrived in England to fly with the Eighth Fighter Command. The 56th Fighter Group, under the command of Colonel Hubert 'Hub' Zemke was stationed initially at King's Cliffe, Northamptonshire, and later at Halesworth, Suffolk, and Boxted, Essex. The men had been trained on, were combat-ready in and seemed quite happy with the P-47. Under the leadership of Hub Zemke, the pilots of the 56th Fighter Group would distinguish themselves and their group as one of the two highest-achieving American fighter outfits of the European air war. Zemke was universally acknowledged as a great fighter pilot, air and ground leader and an outstanding professional soldier. The men of the Fourth Fighter Group admired him as much as those of his own group.

Grover Hall recalled:

To the 4th went the dubious honour of selection as the group to give the Thunderbolt its combat baptism. To the pilots, the Spitfire was a sure-footed, graceful little filly; the P-47, a bull-necked, unwieldy stallion.

There were a lot of little things. The propeller on old model Spits turned counter-clockwise, so they would have to grow accustomed to the different torque of the P-47. They liked the Spits' .20-mm cannon, and saw little sense in the P-47's eight .50 cal. machine-guns. The cannon is larger and more explosive; with cannon a pilot could always see when he got strikes on an enemy plane; it gave the exhilarating feeling of tearing the German to bits. They were not impressed by the fact that the .50 cal. machine-gun bullets had much more range and that many more rounds could be carried in the wings.

The Spit's legs were knock-kneed and close together, while the P-47's were bow-legged and wide apart like a hawk's, so it could land in places the Spit couldn't taxi. The pilots complained that the mirror and glass canopy on the P-47 made it difficult to spot enemy planes. But the chief thing the pilots abhorred about the P-47 was its great size and weight (seven tons). With their radial engines, the craft resembled milk bottles. The pilots missed the jockey feeling the Spit compactness gave. Early model 'T-bolts' had a way of giving off smoke in the cockpit, which fact all but made some pilots bale out. At first, they weren't supposed to go below 18,000 feet in combat with 47s.

The pilots junked the P-47 rear-view mirrors and installed Spit mirrors and bleated, 'If they had to change why couldn't they give us

Mustangs instead of these things? They won't climb, they won't turn tight, they won't do anything but dive.'

Remarks they made about the sponsors of the P-47 were unladylike. Said the P-47 sponsors of the pilots: 'Prima donnas!'

On 10 March 1943 the Fourth Fighter Group gave the P-47 its combat debut. It was planned to be the day that the Germans would first get a look at the wonder plane. All personnel watched the take-off. The pilots got almost to the end of the runway before pulling the stick, wishing to remain on the ground as long as possible. They circled the field. The engines gave off a deep-throated roar, but the distinguishing sound of the P-47 was the whistling noise created by the airflow on its radial engine. Leading the group was Peterson; he set course over Debden and headed for France. They swept down the French coast. To their exquisite relief, the *Luftwaffe* didn't come up. When they returned to base, Peterson, eagle of the Eagles, stated, 'I don't mind telling you, I was scared.'

CHAPTER FIVE

Thunderbolt

On 15 April 1943 Don Blakeslee (who in less than a year would be in command of the Fourth Fighter Group) led ten Thunderbolts as they dived at 23,000 feet to intercept three Fw 190s. Blakeslee pulled within range of one the German fighters and opened fire with his eight .50-calibre guns. The enemy pilot tried to bale out of his stricken machine, but at 500 feet he had waited too long. When Blakeslee was asked later about the kill and the P-47's ability to out-dive the Fw 190, he replied: 'By God, it ought to dive. It certainly won't climb.' It was the first victory by a Thunderbolt.

In the summer of 1943, the Thunderbolts of the Fourth Fighter Group flew sweeps into the European continent with virtual impunity. They tried to tease the enemy into sending up his fighters but the Germans wouldn't play. The Germans were only interested in engaging the Allied bombers and seemed unwilling to fight with the P-47s, unless they were escorting B-17s or B-24s on their bombing raids. Still, the sweeps increased the Debden pilots' experience with the big P-47 and taught them a lot about its peculiarities, shortcomings and potential. Meanwhile, they grew in numbers, in confidence and capability. The Germans countered by withdrawing from the airfields they were using near the Channel, to fields much further inland, often beyond the range of Allied fighters. There, the canny *Luftwaffe* would lie in wait for the moment when the Allied escort fighters reached the limits of their range and were forced to turn back for their English bases. Then, the Fw 190s and Bf 109s would strike at the American heavy bombers.

It didn't take long for the Eighth Fighter Command to counter the German tactic. By fitting a streamlined extra fuel tank under the P-47's belly, the flying and fighting range of the aeroplane could be significantly extended. These tanks could be jettisoned when empty or when the pilot engaged an enemy aircraft in combat. The pilots referred to the drop tanks as 'babies'.

The first time the Germans would see Thunderbolts with their babies was on 28 July 1943. The targets of the Eighth Bomber Command that day were the Fieseler aircraft works at Kassel and other aircraft industrial facilities at Oschersleben. It marked the first occasion that P-47s were able to enter Germany, thanks to their newly extended range capability. Some 123 Thunderbolts of the 4th, 56th and 78th Fighter Groups flew withdrawal support for the bombers.

The plan called for the Thunderbolts to *rendezvous* with the bombers near Emmerich, Germany. When they arrived, the American fighter pilots found that one combat box formation of B-17s was under heavy attack by upwards of sixty Fw 190s and Ju 88s, and one of the crippled bombers was being attacked by six Focke-Wulfs as it struggled to keep up with the bomber formation. The German fighter pilots were shocked to find themselves suddenly under attack, at a point where they had thought they were well beyond any fighter's range. In what seemed mere seconds, nine of the enemy interceptors fell to the guns of the Debden Thunderbolts. In the air battle, the Americans destroyed eighteen enemy aircraft against the loss of just one of their own – Captain Joe Mathews. Mathews baled out, landed safely and managed to evade capture in France. He made it back to Debden, where he claimed one kill before he had been brought down.

As 1943 wore on, the Eighth Air Force steadily grew in strength with the arrival in England of more and more heavy bomber crews and their aircraft, as well as increasing numbers of fighters dedicated mainly to the protection of the bombers. The fighters, mostly Thunderbolts, performed their shepherding duties well, but as the targets of the bombers moved progressively eastward into Germany, the range limitation of the fighters again came into play. The mission of Sunday 10 October is a case in point. The Fourth Fighter Group was assigned to escort the Framlingham-based 390th Bomb Group's B-17s on their trip to hit Munster. Some fifty Thunderbolts accompanied the heavies, but the normally tight defensive formation flown by the bombers was loose and thirty German interceptors rose to attack the bombers as they approached the target. Don Blakeslee was leading the P-47s and they went to work trying to scatter the enemy fighters. However, before they could achieve this the Thunderbolts reached the limit of their combat radius and Blakeslee was forced to radio the B-17s: 'Horseback to big friends. Sorry, we'll have to leave you now.'

The disappointment of the B-17 crewmen must have been acute as they saw their guardian Thunderbolts wheeling through the turn that would put them on a return course for England, leaving only fading vapour trails behind. The bomber boys had been led to believe that their Flying Fortresses could protect themselves by virtue of the many guns they carried and the fields of fire they manifested when tightly packed into their defensive box formations. Now, they would learn the truth – the odds of surviving a tour of duty in the bombers dropped dramatically when the protection of the little friends was removed.

By the autumn of 1943, the *Luftwaffe* knew the range limits of the Allied fighters well and waited until the P-47s had to turn for home before attacking the B-17 formations in force. As it happened, the bomber piloted by Lieutenant John Winant, son of the American ambassador to Britain, was among the first of the B-17s to be shot down that day. Twenty-one-year-old Winant baled out and became a prisoner-of-war. In what seemed only a few minutes, some fifty aircraft of both sides were alight and were down or on their way down to the German soil. As one American airplane commander later put it: 'You could find your way to the target and back by following the fires of the crashed planes.'

The cannon, machine-gun and rocket fire of the attacking German fighters continued relentlessly. Not only did they focus attention on the softer targets – bombers already crippled and straggling – but also they closed in on the lead squadron of B-17s, reducing their number to a single bomber. Even so, the bombers pressed on. In the entire European air war, the bombers of the Eighth Air Force never turned back from a target. The price they were paying in the skies over Munster was steep, however. Many American gunners, navigators, bombardiers and pilots lay wounded and bleeding in their freezing and unpressurised aircraft.

Their bombs were delivered on the target, and the great formations headed back towards England, still largely together. They were met by more fighters, but this time it was Thunderbolts, the first elements of a second effort of Fighter Command to meet and shepherd them back – fresh little friends to guard their charges safely home.

In the air action, the B-17 gunners claimed sixty German fighters shot down. Twenty-five American bombers were downed with their ten-man crews. Of the 313 bombers that had been sent on the raid, 236 had managed to release their bombs in the target area. The escorting Allied fighters had accounted for nineteen enemy fighters downed. After the raid there was a lot of speculation in the Eighth Air Force about the possibility that the Americans might soon be forced to abandon daylight bombing, as both the Germans and the British had done.

Colonel Chesley Peterson had come to Debden with the Eagles and was, perhaps, their most highly decorated veteran. He had commanded the Fourth Fighter Group from August 1943 until January 1944, amassed an enormous number of fighter missions by the end of his command and had been shot down once. He appeared to be showing some signs of strain near the end of his combat flying when his Thunderbolt was hit and he had to parachute into the Channel from less than 1,000 feet. His parachute had failed to open fully. Luckily, he survived. On another occasion he returned to Debden after an air battle and was so exhausted that he was barely able to land the big fighter. It would seem that he had given all he had to give.

After coffee in the officers' mess, Johnny Godfrey and Bob Richards caught a ride in a truck out to the 336th Squadron dispersal hut, where they introduced themselves to their new CO, Major Miley. He checked their logbooks, asked several questions and welcomed them to the squadron. In the hut they met several of the 336th pilots, including Jim Goodson, William Dunn, Willard Millikan and Don Gentile, whom some of the pilots called 'Gentle'. There were two flights in the squadron. A Flight was commanded by Goodson and B Flight by Gentile. In his book *The Look of Eagles*, Johnny Godfrey wrote:

> Both Don and I, of course, never guessed at this first meeting how our lives would eventually intermingle. Many stories were to be written of Don, with me basking in his limelight. The descriptions of him were invariably the same – tall, dark, handsome . . . But no matter how much was written about him, no one put down on paper the true Don.
>
> In an era of swashbuckling, hard-drinking, carousing fighter pilots, Don stood out like a symbol of virtue. His only vice was an occasional cigar. The majority of us lived from day to day; Don was just the opposite. Every payday most of his month's pay was sent home to be banked in his account. Don had been born of immigrant parents, and maybe for this reason an ambition boiled inside of him to prove his capabilities to the world. The hard shell about him was very seldom broken. To deviate from his appointed task seemed to him a weakness. Sometimes I was able to observe, through an occasional crack in this shell, a different Don, one who could suffer spells of depression and who knew his human limitations. These cracks didn't show very often though, and like a turtle sensing danger, Don would retreat once more into his armour. In the air, however, it was different.

Johnny and Bob went along on a practice mission and afterwards learnt that they were scheduled to fly on their first actual combat mission the next day, 27 September 1943. Neither of them got much sleep that night and were bleary-eyed when their batman woke them for the 6:30 am briefing. As it was a mission day, the pilots were treated to ham and eggs for breakfast, during which Johnny thought about the fact that it was two years and one month since he had enlisted in the Royal Canadian Air Force. He had more than 400 hours of flight time in his logbook and now, at long last, he was about to go on his first real mission. Outside the mess, the trucks waited to take the pilots to the operations building for briefing.

At the far end of the large room was a raised platform like a stage and on it a very large map of England and the European continent. On the map a red line had been drawn from Debden to Essen at the head of the Ruhr Valley in Germany. When the Colonel marched into the room, all the pilots rose to attention until he put them at their ease. They sat and he spoke:

We will be target support for four boxes of B-17s. We should arrive over the target area at 0830 hours. In case anyone gets lost, steer 260 for Debden. Intelligence reports moderate to heavy flak over the target. We will fly at 26,000 feet. Press [start engines] time is 0715. Any questions?'

There were a few and then Peterson added: 'Synchronise your watches. It is now 0644; in 50 seconds it will be 0645 – five, four, three, two, one, zero. Swoop will fill you in on the weather.' Five minutes later everyone headed for the trucks that would take them out to dispersal, where they quickly dressed in flying gear and their Mae West life jackets. Each man received an escape kit and a chocolate bar. A board on the wall indicated that Johnny was to fly as Number Two in Blue Section, wingman to Blue Leader, Don.

There was almost no conversation in the room now; there was only an occasional quiet exchange between a pilot and his crew chief. The relatively short while until it was time to head out to the planes seemed an eternity for Johnny and he was relieved when they all left the room. He now met Larry Krantz, his crew chief, who helped him to strap in and get settled in the cockpit of his P-47, coded VF-P. Krantz wished him good luck and Johnny nodded at Don Gentile who sat across the dispersal in VF-Q, the aeroplane Don had named *Donnie Boy*. They started their engines and, in the prescribed order, taxied out onto the perimeter track. Johnny followed Don.

Once airborne, the lengthy forming-up procedure began, until all forty-eight Thunderbolts had assembled themselves into flights, sections, squadrons and the group. As they neared the Channel, the order came to spread out slightly from the tight formation they had been flying, relieving Johnny of the intense concentration he had been exercising in order to maintain tight formation on Don's plane. They entered battle formation. Bob Richards was up ahead, flying as Red Two on Jim Goodson.

At that moment Johnny was startled by a loud whine in his earphones. The Germans were trying to jam the American fighter radio frequencies, something they frequently attempted but rarely achieved. Now he got his first sight of flak. They were entering enemy territory and the Germans were putting up a lot of the harmless-looking but deadly little black puffs of smoke and the group could do nothing but fly through it. They could try taking evasive action by weaving, but as no one could predict where the next burst would occur, it was senseless. The excitement of the experience caused Johnny to gulp oxygen almost as though he were hyperventilating. He forced himself to stay focused on keeping near Don. He was as frightened as he had ever been, but at the same time thoroughly exhilarated. Then he heard a voice over the R/T: 'There go the bombs.' Johnny couldn't even spot the bombers. Where the hell were they? Another voice on the R/T. It was Blakeslee this time: 'This is Horseback. All planes return to base.' They had only been escorting the bombers for twenty minutes. It had seemed much longer. They passed another large group of P-47s overhead, on their way to shepherd the bombers back to the Channel coast. Johnny was calmer now; he was able to consider what had happened in the past moments. He was staggered by the realisation that his two years of training had not really prepared him for what he had just experienced. He was still learning and would continue to do so in the months to come.

Approaching the Channel, the group began to let down from 26,000 feet. Seemingly impenetrable cloud masses were building up ahead of the Thunderbolts and Johnny heard the squadron leader call for a tighter formation. Section by section, the planes entered the cloud. He stuck as close to Don as he dared and, to his relief, they were able to keep each other in sight. The turbulence was severe in the cloud though, and Johnny had to fight the controls to keep the big fighter stable. To his even greater relief, they finally broke out of the cloud mass and saw the Channel coast just off to their right. Don then called him on the R/T to say that he was low on fuel and would land at the nearest airdrome he could find. He told Johnny to follow him in. They soon spotted an airfield, Bradwell, in Essex, and quickly landed there. They taxied to the control tower and parked. Don arranged for their planes to be refuelled while Johnny had a cigarette. When Don returned, he remarked: 'Boy, that was a close one. We pretty near spun in. When we hit that bumpy air my gyro toppled and I lost my instruments. It's a darned good thing the cloud base was at 1,500 feet, otherwise we'd be flying submarines at the bottom of the Channel.' Johnny was flabbergasted. 'I'll be damned. I thought there was something screwy on your letdown, but figured you had a tricky way of doing it. Well, we made it anyway.'

From the diary of 1st Lt Jack Raphael, 336th Fighter Squadron:

5 January 1944 – Briefed at 09:30 for a show south of Paris. I was leading spare section with Dutch Van Wyk as my wingman. Started rolling OK on take-off, but suddenly began to swerve toward the left. Tried to correct for the swing, but had no control. Going too fast to stop, so I tried to get off the deck. Herter's old clunk didn't have enough power. Chopped the throttle and hit WE-K, shearing off its starboard wing and chopping up the tail. My wheels were torn off and I skidded on, finally cartwheeling just short of six 500 lb bombs. Wasn't injured except for banging up my shin a little. Both VF-R and WD-K written off. LUCKY! Gentile and Messenger each got an Fw 190 and Godfrey damaged another. Had an aircraft rec. test and put in an hour of Link.

There was a day in January when all three squadrons of the group were sent to escort bombers to a target in the Paris area. A fight was on and Don had shot down an Fw 190 and was in position and firing on a second. He watched as the German fighter dived into the ground in flames. He then pulled out and began the long climb back up to rejoin his squadron. But as he climbed he found himself alone, having become separated from his wingman. With no warning, the orange fireballs of Fw 190 cannon fire came flashing over his upturned port wing. Reefing the big Thunderbolt over, he tried to out-turn the Fw 190 at that low altitude, just as if he were flying his old Spitfire, with little concern about spinning out. He now became aware of a second Fw 190, the wingman of his current adversary. The three of them zigged, zagged and tore over the treetops, all trying to out-turn their enemy. In frustration or fear, or both, Don yelled over the R/T: 'Help! Help! I'm being clobbered!' Somewhere, high above him, he heard Willard Millikan drawl: 'Now, if you will tell me your call sign and approximate position we'll send help.' Soon, one of the German planes was no longer in the chase, a victim of the I-can-turn-tighter-than-you-can game, but the other hung on relentlessly. As hard as he tried, Don could not shake him or manoeuvre into position to shoot him. Much later at Debden, one of the pilots wrote a song, to the tune of Tramp, tramp, tramp, the boys are marching.

Help, help, help, I'm being clobbered,
Down here by the railroad track,
Two 190s chase me 'round
And we're damn near to the ground.
Tell them I got two if I don't make it back!

Johnny had given his crew chief £2 to have an artist paint a name and a picture of Lucky looking out of a horseshoe on the nose of VF-P, his own P-47. He named the aircraft *Reggie's Reply* to honour his late brother. One day he was assigned to fly as spare man as far as the enemy coast, and if none of the squadron pilots turned back, he was to return to base. As the Thunderbolts of the 336th Fighter Squadron approached the German side of the Channel coast, Green Two turned back for Debden with a mechanical problem. Johnny slipped into position next to Jim Goodson, Green One. They were flying at 26,000 feet towards an immense cloud formation rising to more than 30,000 feet. The squadron knifed into the cloud and when they emerged, they had completely split up and were scattered over a wide area.

Johnny saw this as an opportunity to dive down and look around for a German fighter or two. In the chaos he thought he wouldn't be missed. When he reached a flight level about 10,000 feet below the squadron, which had just rendezvoused with the bomber stream, he levelled off and was amazed to spot a lone Bf 109 beneath and ahead of him. He considered the situation and accepted that he was simply too inexperienced to risk a dogfight with the German and decided to follow the enemy plane and come up underneath it for an attack.

At 12,000 feet he again began levelling off and was now 500 feet below the German. In the dive his airspeed had increased to more than 500 mph and he acted to bleed off some of that speed as he worked to position the Thunderbolt about 200 yards behind the enemy fighter. The German continued on a straight and steady course, unaware of Johnny's presence. When the Bf 109 filled his gunsight, Johnny pressed the gun button on the control stick, his plane shuddered and almost instantly a great flame erupted and engulfed the little Messerschmitt. A debris cloud appeared behind it and enveloped the Thunderbolt. For a split second Johnny worried that the junk might break his windscreen.

It was then that it hit him. He described it later as a strange exhilaration mixed with a horrible feeling of remorse that overcame him.

I'd destroyed my first plane, and undoubtedly killed a man – I trusted that God would understand. I flew, unscathed, through the smithereens of what was a plane and a man, and banking sharply I cleared my tail and watched the clouds hungrily suck the falling debris into their bosom. The wind dispersed the fast disappearing black cloud, and I flew alone.

In full throttle, Johnny began a protracted climb. The reaction to having shot down his first plane hit him hard, causing his hands to tremble and making it difficult to hold the stick steady. The big fighter jumped and jittered as it climbed. It occurred to him that if a plane could be shot down that easily, he might well be the next guy brought down. He twisted continuously, checking every part of the sky for enemy aircraft. He worried about the blind spot to his rear and jinked to get a quick look back that way.

Behind and roughly 2,000 feet below, another Bf 109 appeared from the heavy cloud. Johnny soon forgot his fear as he racked the P-47 over to the left in a tight, diving turn that would position him behind this new German. He set up an approach similar to his earlier encounter, hoping for a double. But this enemy pilot was far more alert and ready for the threat. The German whipped his Messerschmitt right and struggled to climb and Johnny strained to stay with him in the extreme turn. As the G forces increased on his body, Johnny fought to stop himself from blacking out. He managed to get the German in his gunsight for an instant and squeezed off some shots. They struck one of the Bf 109's wings, ripping loose a two-foot-long section of panelling. He tried again, striving to aim his bullets into the cockpit of the enemy fighter, but just at that moment the German broke off the chase and went into the nearby cloud cover. Exhausted, Johnny turned for Debden.

As Johnny taxied the Thunderbolt onto the hardstand, his crew chief, Larry Krantz, was elated to see that the tape over the muzzles of his guns was shot through and blackened, and that his pilot had scored his first victory. 'Thanks, Lieutenant. You just won me £5 in the pool the crew chiefs had for the first plane to be shot down this month.'

That evening, as Johnny was buying drinks for everyone in the bar, Colonel Peterson came in and congratulated him. 'Lieutenant, could I have a word with you in private?' Johnny followed him out into the hallway. Peterson said: 'Lieutenant, I want to tell you this in private, so as not to embarrass you in front of your friends. I want all my pilots to finish their tours. What you did today was very foolhardy and risky; for this reason I cannot condone it. In the future stay with the group, and if you want to go on a bounce, make sure that somebody is with you.'

Don Gentile recalled:

Making a fighter pilot is a long business. My instructors had worked hard back home, and when I was graduated I was graded 'better than average pilot'. But flying an airplane is only part of fighting with one, and most of the other part a man has to learn in actual combat. He has to learn from his fellow soldiers, and from the enemy.

I was lucky enough to get attached to the Eagle Squadron, in which some of the finest fighter pilots who ever lived were working – lucky enough to get into the war at a time when a man could afford to be cautious about learning and could feel his way and not just have to throw himself against the enemy and try to clout him down blindly.

I learned a lot from the enemy, too. In the beginning we were up against Goering's Abbeville Kids – those yellow-nosed Focke-Wulf, veteran big-timers. There were not many better teachers of attack and defence than those killers, and of those who were better teachers quite a few were in the Eagle Squadron.

There are two things a fighter pilot must have to do his work in combat and that he can't really acquire anywhere else except in combat: confidence in his ability to kill and confidence in his ability to get away when in trouble.

If you feel you can kill and feel they can't kill you, then you'll have the offensive spirit. Without that offensive spirit – ability to lunge instantaneously and automatically like a fighting cock at the enemy the moment you spot him – you are lost. You either 'go along for the ride', as we call it when a fellow hangs back and doesn't make kills, or eventually you get shot down.

I know, because it took me quite a long time to build up confidence in myself, which I had thought I had when I left home, and there was quite a long time when I went along just for the ride.

I started . . . by picking the best man I could get to fly on my wing – Johnny Godfrey, of Woonsocket, R.I., who doesn't like Germans. They killed his brother, Reggie, at sea, and the name Johnny has painted on his plane is *Reggie's Reply*. He means it, too. The point about him is that he not only is a fierce, brave boy, but he knows his business as well.

Teamwork is the answer to any man's score, but in the meantime there was plenty of competition within the team. Once a battle started there were a great many of the boys who saw in it what I saw – the chance to make a record that would come in handy later in life.

One of the best of them was Captain B [Beeson]. We were entirely unlike as people and came from different backgrounds as well as different parts of the country. But the odd thing is that he had the same idea as I and he had the same drive. He had had to quit on the eve of going to college, as I had, and for the same reason, and had joined the RAF for the same reason as I, because he felt flying would give him the best chance to survive the war and to make a record in it that would provide a leg up on a peacetime career.

Our scores mounted side by side. We flew every mission. One day he'd be ahead of me and the next day I would be ahead of him, and the first question each of us asked when landing was how much had the other fellow got.

Ground-crew men who could not understand the confidence each of us had in himself and who understood only the dangers of our work were a little puzzled by our attitude, I imagine. I remember one day early this month when I went up, under orders, to London to make a radio broadcast. I was a little sore about it until I saw it was raining and I said what was in my mind. 'Well, I guess I won't miss anything today,' I said, and the faces of the ground-crew men around me looked bewildered for a moment, and then they started to laugh. But it was just that while they understood the dangers they did not understand a man feeling completely able to handle those dangers.

On Thursday, April 5th, Captain B had twenty-one German planes destroyed to his credit and I had twenty-two. We went out to strafe some airports, and this is the kind of work all of us like the least. It is the most dangerous. A man can't rely on himself to carry him through. When he commits himself to an attack against a ground target protected by flak, he just throws his plane at it and the rest is luck. But this is necessary work – if the Germans won't fight in their planes in the air they have to be fought on the ground.

Captain B had bad luck at one airport, while I was having good luck at another. He destroyed two Nazi ships and then I heard him over the radio saying flak had started glycol leaking out of him and he was gaining altitude. He said nothing after that for quite a while.

Although he was only twenty-two years old, he was a man of great composure and he believed in radio discipline. After that long silence he said in that soft, quiet, quick voice of his, 'I am baling out'. And that was all he said – no goodbyes, no sorrys; nothing, just radio discipline.

That was the day my score ran up to twenty-seven destroyed. I didn't realise it until I put in my claim for five on the ground that I had seen burn, and Lieut. Grover C. Hall, Jr said, 'Well, Don, that makes you the man who has destroyed more German planes than any American in two wars'.

I asked him if he knew Captain B had gone down, and he hurried off at once to B's squadron. Mess was very quiet that night. Captain B's squadron had scheduled a party, and they went through with it, but nobody's heart was in it and the girls who had come a long way to dance must have thought the Americans were just lumps.

A man likes to have a good score, but our training teaches us how important teamwork is, and the fellow who values his private score over his team either learns fast or goes down.

As he got to know Don Gentile better, Johnny came to like and respect him as a fighter pilot and as a man.

I found in Don Gentile a section leader who knew my capabilities and had faith in my eyesight. He was aggressive, which I liked, but having had so much more experience, he served as a check to my recklessness. The first two German planes that he destroyed were shot down while with the RAF at Dieppe in 1942. He had destroyed two more with the USAAF, and one more would make him an ace. He was quiet on the ground, but once he stepped into the cockpit of a plane his manner changed completely. Gone were the suppressions and fears that often plagued him, and he flew his plane with complete competence.

On the day Gentile downed his fifth enemy aircraft, Johnny congratulated him.

Teamwork when properly used was a potent offensive weapon . . . I was envious of Don's accomplishments. If I could only shoot down two more planes this month I would have accomplished in four months what had taken him much longer; but thinking it over, this teamwork idea might work out to both our advantages.

After more than a month living in house number 7, a room in the officers' mess became available for Johnny and Bob. But it was with some reluctance that they packed their things and moved, with Lucky, to room 22 on the second floor of the mess. It was certain that Lucky would be a problem. The executive officer, Colonel Clatinoff, had made a hard and fast rule that no dogs were allowed in the mess. Several of the pilots owned dogs and all of them, including Lucky, enjoyed running around in the large lounge, but Clatinoff was not amused. He ordered that any offending animal should be rounded up and put in jail. The owner would then have to pay a five-shilling fine to bail the pooch out. Johnny and Bob did their best to keep Lucky out of Clatinoff's sight. By day the dog had the run of the 336th Fighter Squadron dispersal hut and at night, the boys kept him in their room, unknown to the Colonel. Many times, when Johnny returned from a mission, Bob would be there, waiting to greet him at the hardstand with Lucky in his arms.

One day Johnny landed at Debden after a rough mission to be met by Bob who told him that once again Clatinoff had put Lucky in jail. Johnny hitched a ride over to the Colonel's office and, after being made to wait for a while, was ushered in to see the exec. Without saying a word, Johnny handed over five-shillings to cover the fine. 'Lieutenant, if this continues I'm going to raise the fine to ten shillings, to impress upon you pilots that the officers' mess is for officers, not dogs. See what you can do to curb Lucky's infractions of my rules, and wipe that smile off your face.' The guardhouse MP accepted Lucky's release slip and walked back to the cells to free the dog. 'One prisoner being released. This one is the most dangerous of the lot. Of all the dogs on the base, he has the rare distinction of having the most arrests. Here, Lucky, your parole officer has arrived.' For the most part, life at Debden had become routine for Johnny and Bob. Johnny spent much of his ground time in the squadron dispersal hut with Lucky and the pilots he had come to know. He had developed an understanding of their strengths and weaknesses and, since the accession of Blakeslee as group commander, had been pleased at the way the Fourth Fighter Group had grown to be much more aggressive and spirited in its operations against the *Luftwaffe*.

Bob, too, had settled in nicely. As an accomplished saxophone player, he became a member of the base orchestra, the only officer in the eight-man combo. They played for the dance party the group staged to the delight of all the revellers that New Year's Eve. The festivities ended with a bang early the next morning when one of the pilots broke into the duty officer's room in the control tower and appropriated a box of flares and rockets, which he then ignited in front of the officers' mess. It was his way of wishing everyone a happy new year.

On 1 January 1944, Don Blakeslee became commander of the Fourth Fighter Group and would lead them in combat on most of their missions through that year. By the time Blakeslee took over the group, most of the Eagle alumni were gone from Debden, due either to rotation or enemy action. Some of the Eagle big names did remain, however, including Don Gentile, Duane Beeson, Bud Care, Jim Clark and Steve Pisanos.

When Blakeslee took charge he left no doubt in anyone's mind about his intentions.

The Fourth Fighter Group is going to be the top fighter group in the Eighth Air Force. We are here to fight. To those who don't believe me I would suggest transferring to another group. I'm going to fly the ass off each one of you. Those who keep up with me, good; those who don't, I don't want them anyway.

From the diary of 1st Lt Jack Raphael, 336th Fighter Squadron:

9 January 1944 – Released until dawn on the 10th. Took VF-M out over Orford Ness to test the guns. All rounds fired but an ejector on one of the guns broke. Came back to Debden on the deck. Nice ride, but 10/10 at 1500. Played some basketball after lunch. After supper George and I came home early. Wrote a letter and studied French for a couple of hours.

CHAPTER SIX

Chums

From the diary of 1st Lt Jack Raphael, 336th Fighter Squadron:

14 January 1944 – Had a freelance to Margny. Flew Green 2. Group got 10 Fw 190s for no losses. 334 got five and 336 got the other five. Gentile got two, Richards one, Garrison one and Garry and Norley shared the other. 334's were shot down by Montgomery, Biel, Whelan, Beeson and Rafalovich. Thoroughly good show! Free beer in the mess. Gentile got a 20 mm in the wing, but nobody else was hit. A batch of Marauders from Chipping Ongar sat down because their base was closed in. Was scheduled for night flying, but tail light was U/S [unserviceable] so it was cancelled. Went to the flicks and took advantage of some of the free beer before hitting the hay.

The pilots of the Fourth Fighter Group lived two to a room in the Debden officers' mess. Johnny Godfrey shared a room with Bob Richards. Don Gentile's roommate was Steve Pisanos. Like Don, Steve had been an Eagle pilot. He had met Don just before the Eagles were transferred from the RAF into the USAAF and they immediately became friends. They dined and drank together in the officers' mess, went to movies on base and to the chapel on Sundays. They also went on weekend passes together and double-dated girls in London on the rare occasions when Don would go on leave. They had become roommates after Steve's previous roommate, Captain Donald Willis, had been transferred to Headquarters, Eighth Fighter Command.

Don remembered:

Steve was just the opposite from me. He was full of vinegar, always talking, laughing, and stirring up something around here. I guess one of the things that made us so close in spite of the differences between us was that we both had Old Country backgrounds and thought America the finest place on earth. Also, we both put flying above everything else.

Steve Pisanos came from Athens originally. By the time he was eleven, he had fallen in love with aircraft and was absolutely committed to becoming an aviator. As he grew older he realised that lacking the money, qualifications and connections needed to gain entry into the prestigious Greek Air Force Academy, he would have to find another way to become a pilot. He then decided to go to America and learn to fly there. Aged eighteen, he attempted to stow away on the Italian liner, *Rex*, when it visited the port of Piraeus, bound for New York. He impersonated a porter carrying luggage and steamer trunks aboard the vessel, but was spotted by the union foreman who questioned his presence and immediately had the harbour police escort him from the ship.

Chastened, but undeterred, Steve, with the help of his elder brother, managed to secure a job a few months later aboard a Greek freighter, as an assistant fireman, a position he knew nothing about. He grabbed the opportunity in the hope that one day the ship would sail into an American port. Luck was with him and, after a stop at Oran to load a cargo of iron ore; the ship proceeded to Baltimore. He had no money, no friends and he spoke no English, but he made it to New York and got a job as a pantry boy at Hatchitt's restaurant, 149th Street at Broadway. It was summer 1938, and Steve was earning the princely sum of $15 a week. After a spell of taking flying lessons at $12 a lesson, he learned of less costly flight instruction in New Jersey and was soon working as a pantry boy at the Park Hotel in Plainfield. He achieved his ambition, became an Eagle and, in October 1942, under the provisions of the modified overseas naturalisation law, became an American citizen. He recalled:

> Sometimes I think of those people who laughed because the pantry boy wanted to fly. I'm not much, I know, but it gives me pleasure to think I came to America with $8 and couldn't even speak the language – and now I'm an officer of the United States Army. I don't care who knows, boy – I'm proud of that, I tell you, boy!

On meeting Don, Steve learned that his new friend had also been excited at the prospect of aviation and learning to fly from an early age. Don told Steve how he had pestered his father to take him over to the Waco factory airport at Troy, Ohio, near his home town of Piqua, so he could watch the biplanes fly there.

Patsy, Don's father, owned and operated a bar and grill in Piqua and when Don reached the age of sixteen, his father let him wait on tables there, paying him a small salary that was significantly augmented by the tips he earned. By his seventeenth birthday, Don had taken that first flight, in an open-cockpit aeroplane. Impressed with how hard his son worked at the bar and grill, Patsy began to accept Don's genuine desire to learn to fly and gave him extra money to take flying lessons. After he soloed, Don was overcome with a need to have his own aeroplane and began begging his father to buy one for him. Patsy objected strenuously. Undeterred, Don took the hard earned $300 that he had saved and bought a small biplane from a man at the Troy airport. As Don recalled, the news spread quickly around Piqua and his mother received a phone call from a neighbour, telling her of Don's purchase and that he was going to kill himself because the plane was no good. Don's mother ranted and raved at him about it as they drove out to the airport. There, they found that the man who had sold him the biplane had flown off with the plane and Don's $300. 'My mother was mad as hell because I had lost the $300 and said, "Son, let that be a lesson to you".'

As that episode slipped into the past, Don resumed urging his father to finance his purchase of another aeroplane. After more months of cajoling, Patsy eventually relented and bought him a single-seater Aerosport biplane, to the great displeasure of Don's mother. In time, she too came around to a grudging acceptance of his intentions. Don recalled:

When I flew around, I buzzed everything on the ground – girl friends' houses, football fields and even a police car, not realising what it was. After that my father threatened to take the plane away from me, which curbed my dare-devil tendencies.

By 1940, Don had earned his private pilot's licence and accumulated considerable flying time. He desperately wanted to join the Aviation Cadet Program of the US Army but lacked the two years of college that the service required of applicants. Later, he heard that the RAF was recruiting American civilian pilots in Cleveland. He drove there and made contact with the Clayton Knight Committee people and submitted his application. Two months later he had been accepted and was sent to California for a refresher course at the Polaris Flight Academy, which Steve had also attended.

At Debden, Steve and Don often talked about aerial combat and what each would do if he found himself in a certain situation. Don related a particular experience that he had had on a mission.

We were still flying Spitfires on this mission and I happened to sight a lone enemy aircraft below our formation. I reported the enemy plane to my leader and, by the time I had manoeuvred my Spit in position to fire, another guy from my squadron was shooting at the enemy aircraft I was after. There was no doubt that during the early days, fighter pilots were eager to get a kill, regardless of the circumstances when a mission was over enemy territory. After that, whenever I sighted an enemy aircraft, I would first break away from the formation and while on the way down, I would report the position of the enemy aircraft.

Ultimately, however, Gentile came to believe that to be successful in air fighting, you had to work as a team and that individualism had no future in aerial combat because of the way the Germans operated in the Second World War. He came to recognise that teamwork with a wingman was the way to survive and become an ace. Attacking the enemy when alone was an invitation to disaster. Air leaders in both the RAF and the USAAF continually emphasised the importance of teamwork as being the only way to beat the Germans in the air. The element leader should do the shooting while the wingman protected his leader's tail. For most of the time that they flew together, whoever spotted an enemy aircraft first, and was in the best position to attack, took the lead with the other covering his 6 o'clock position. This tactic and method was later copied by American fighter pilots in the Vietnam War.

Steve Pisanos knew and admired Johnny Godfrey too. He recalls:

Johnny Godfrey was twenty-one years old when he joined the Fourth Fighter Group in the middle of September 1943, as a second lieutenant. Godfrey was assigned to B Flight, the 336th Squadron. B Flight was led by Don Gentile. Both men were over six feet tall, good-looking with well-trimmed 'Errol Flynn' moustaches. Godfrey was, in his own words, a sort of rebellious guy at home. His parents wanted him to go to college after high school, but he refused to get involved in further studies.

After Johnny's first combat mission, a Ramrod [bomber escort mission] to Essen in which he flew as Don's wingman, Don told Steve in the bar that evening that he was quite impressed by Johnny's flying ability and by his exceptionally keen eyesight. Probably more than any other factor, it was Johnny's incredible eyesight that singled him out from nearly all the other pilots in the group, and maybe the entire air force. Invariably, he was the first to spot the speck that grew into an enemy plane. He said that he thought Johnny was going to be an excellent wingman, as he was eager, alert and a very smooth pilot.

Some time later, following the mission to Solingen on 1 December 1943, when Johnny had broken away from the formation to find and down a Bf 109, and was later reprimanded by Colonel Peterson for violating group rules, Johnny confided in Don. He said that he had come over to England to shoot down enemy planes, that neither Colonel Peterson nor anyone else was going to stop him. If he wanted to risk his own life that was his business. Don tried to persuade Johnny that he would have to change his perspective if he wanted to survive his tour. During another mission, when he was flying Don's wing, Johnny began to see the sense in what Don had said to him. As a team that day they each destroyed an Fw 190 and damaged another. Steve believes that that mission in particular convinced Johnny that teamwork was indeed the answer to success and survival in aerial fighting. After that, the pair were busy perfecting the wingman approach. Don's account of that mission is as follows:

> John and I had been separated from the others in my flight and suddenly, as we turned around to look for some of our boys, I spotted these two lone Fw 190s cruising along. I told Godfrey, 'Let's go and jump these two guys before they get away'. We turned and dived on them and as we got close behind them I said to John, 'I'll take the one to the left and you take the guy on the right' and that's how we clobbered them. After we parked our Jugs I asked John what he thought about his second kill. He said: 'Perfect teamwork. I liked it'.

Don knew Johnny had seen the light.

Steve added:

> I believe that the January 5th 1944 mission to Tours, France, in which Gentile and Godfrey got two more Fws, was the birth of the legendary Gentile-Godfrey team in the Fourth Fighter Group, that was to cause so much havoc for the *Luftwaffe* in the days ahead. Thereafter, the pair worked harmoniously together, shooting down the enemy in droves.
>
> Each night Don and I analysed and evaluated the mission we had flown that day, considering our mistakes and those of the bomber boys, and the excessive chatter of some of our guys over the R/T, which was something our Group Commander, Don Blakeslee, did not tolerate. We talked about the different tactics and techniques of air fighting, taking advantage of the sun in getting ready to jump an

opponent, attacking a stationary or moving train and the element of surprise when attacking a ground target. We agreed completely on the importance of making only one pass when strafing parked aircraft on an airdrome, because any additional passes, regardless of the direction of your approach, will inevitably draw fire from the drome defence gunners who will then be waiting for you. Don mentioned too, how he had learned to admire and respect the capabilities of other pilots in the 336th Squadron and how impressed he was with the talents of John Godfrey as a fighter pilot. He talked too about his belief that, you had to prepare yourself for air combat by studying and learning all there is to know about the rules of the game because, when you find yourself in the midst of an aerial duel, there is no time to stop and think about what you should do. If you stop to think about it, you will not have time to act. He believed that it was essential for a fighter pilot to know the capabilities of his own aircraft by heart, as well as those of the machine his enemy is flying.

In January both Don and Steve had downed five enemy aircraft and become aces. By then, the ace race among the pilots of all the American fighter groups in the ETO was on with a vengeance. The Eighth Fighter Command had decreed that enemy aircraft destroyed on the ground would now be credited the same as those destroyed in the air. Both Johnny and Don were determined to destroy as many German aircraft as they possibly could and each had a specific goal in mind. Don wanted to break Eddie Rickenbacker's First World War score of twenty-six enemy aircraft destroyed, while Johnny was out to down fifty of the enemy's planes. As the pair flew more and more missions together, Johnny flying as wingman to Don, they became increasingly efficient at killing the enemy. Johnny learned a lot about air fighting from Don, and both men continued to pile up amazing tallies. Working together, supporting and protecting each other in the air, they soon achieved a kind of celebrity status, both in the group and beyond.

On the mission to Bordeaux on 5 March 1944, Steve Pisanos was forced to crash-land and spent the next six months evading the *Gestapo* in Paris. While there, he lived and worked with the Resistance, harassing military convoys and sabotaging German occupation facilities. When the Allies liberated Paris on 26 August, he and many other Allied airmen who had been hiding in the capital, were able to make their way back to England.

On 3 May 1943 *The Stars and Stripes* featured a front page photo of 1st Lieutenant Spiros 'Steve' Pisanos taking the oath of allegiance to the United States before the US Commissioner in London.

Yesterday, 1st Lt Spiros 'Steve' Pisanos, of Athens, Greece, and Plainfield, New Jersey, became the first American soldier in the British Isles to become a US citizen under the provisions of the modified overseas naturalization law. He was sworn in by Dr Henry Hazard in London. In 1938, Steve Pisanos landed in New York with $8 and no knowledge of English. Among other things, he was determined to fly. He got a job for $15 a week. He spent $12 of it for every hour of flying instruction he received at a flying school. In 1941, with a private pilot's license, he joined the RAF. He has been in 19 operations with the RAF and the US Fighter Squadron to which he was transferred in October. Said Steve, 'This is the most happiest day of my life'.

That evening, the following sign was displayed at the bar in the Debden officers' mess: 'FREE BEER ON STEVE PISANOS – AMERICAN.'

On 8 March 1944, Johnny became an ace. The group had been sent to Germany on another escort mission. The target was the VKF ball-bearing works at Erkner and the bomber force was made up of 411 B-17s and 209 B-24s. They would be escorted by 876 fighters. The bulk of the enemy fighter opposition would be the single-engined Bf 109s and Fw 190s, as much of the *Luftwaffe*'s twin-engined fighter fleet had been put out of action in February and early March by the American fighters. The bombing results this day were good, thanks in no small measure to the efforts of the American fighter pilots.

The squadron experienced a lot of malfunctions on the way and several pilots were forced to turn back to base. While Johnny had taken off as a section leader in command of three other aircraft, it wasn't long before all three had aborted. Don, in charge of another section, soon found himself in the same situation, and Johnny joined up with him as Red Two. So few Fourth Fighter Group pilots were still airborne that they dropped the use of call signs for this mission and used each other's first names over the R/T.

As they approached the bomber stream, they saw a number of enemy fighters attacking and diving through the bomber formations. The sky around them seemed full of fire, debris and opening parachutes. They entered the area of the battle with Don yelling for Johnny to cover him as he dived on a German fighter. Wingman followed leader into the attack, checking first to ensure their 6 o'clock position was clear. Knowing he was well protected, Don quickly got into firing position behind the German and efficiently blew him apart. Now it was Johnny's turn, as another Bf 109 slipped into his ring sight. He heard Don say that they were still clear and for him to nail the German, which he did. The Messerschmitt flipped on its back, trailing smoke through its final plunge. The two pilots formed abreast and climbed for the fighter formation at 28,000 feet, slightly above the bomber stream. As they arrived, they noticed two Bf 109s turning in to attack the B-17s and dived to shoot them. Don took the German aircraft on the left, which burst into flames after a few seconds' attention from the American. Don and Johnny had begun firing simultaneously and Johnny excitedly watched as his Bf 109 exploded in mid-air. Neither German pilot could have survived.

Now they were flying at the same altitude as the bombers. The enemy fighter attacks had ceased and the sky in that area soon filled with black flak bursts. At that moment Don checked his 6 o'clock high and spotted a lone Messerschmitt Bf 109 dropping down on them. He yelled 'break' and turned hard left as Johnny turned sharply right. The alert German pilot managed to gain the advantage in a tailchase against Johnny. Don, meanwhile, was trying to get on the tail of the German, who then broke off and headed for the ground. They followed him down and when the German pulled out, Johnny got on his tail and squeezed off some rounds at him, noting the strikes on his fuselage and wing as they skimmed the treetops. Then Johnny's ammunition ran out and he called for Don to finish off the enemy plane.

Later, Don reported:

I was flying Red 1 when the combat started; at the time Lt Godfrey and I were alone and we went down to break up a head-on attack on the lead box of Forts by a large gaggle of Bf 109s. There were about fifty 109s in the area flying in twos and fours. I picked out two and we did six or seven turns with them. Lt Godfrey got one. He had a hard time turning without flaps, but when I used them I closed in to 75 yards and clobbered him. He rolled over and went down streaming white smoke. He was spiralling out of control and almost obscured by smoke. We attacked another 109 head-on. Using combat flaps I got line astern on him, closed to 100 yards, got good strikes and saw the pilot baled out. I then noticed two 109s flying almost abreast and close together. I told Lt Godfrey to take the one on the right and I took the one on the left. I opened fire at 250 yards and closed in until I almost rammed him. I got good strikes. The plane went down spinning and smoking badly and the pilot baled out. Lt Godfrey's e/a [enemy aircraft] exploded.

Then Lt Godfrey was attacked from 4 o'clock. We turned into him and got him between us. I fired first and got strikes but overshot, so I told Lt Godfrey to take over. He got strikes but ran out of ammunition. I told him to cover me while I finished him off. His belly tank caught fire and he went down to 1,000 feet and baled out.

During this combat many 109s were in the area and we were able to pick the best bounces. It was the way that Lt Godfrey stayed with me in every manoeuvre that made our success possible.

On the return trip they encountered a lone B-17 with one of its engines shut down. For a full hour the pair escorted the crippled bomber back to England.

Don claimed three Bf 109s destroyed and one shared with Johnny, who claimed two Bf 109s destroyed and his half of a third aircraft shared with Gentile.

After buying drinks for everyone that evening, Johnny sat with a glass of wine and Lucky on his lap in his room. A visitor arrived, Charlotte Fredericks, the attractive brunette nurse that Bob had dated a few times. She asked Johnny if he was going to the base dance that night. She said that she and some other nurses had just moved into a tent hospital three miles from Debden and had been invited to the dance. Johnny decided he would go too.

The first meeting of Don Blakeslee and Freddie Glover was, according to Grover Hall, inauspicious, to say the least. In fact, after being introduced to Colonel Blakeslee in the bar on the evening of his arrival at Debden, Glover didn't even bother to unpack his uniforms. Before coming to the Fourth Fighter Group, Glover had been a ferry pilot, delivering P-38 fighters, and had no combat experience. Blakeslee seemed unimpressed and Glover climbed on the offensive: 'Well, I think I can fly a plane as good as anybody else I see around here – SIR!' To which the Blakeslee responded: 'Have a drink.' 'I've had a drink,' said the new man. Thereafter, Blakeslee discovered that Glover was one of the few pilots there who loved fighting the Germans as much as he did, and the two got along very well.

Freddie Glover had played professional baseball in civilian life and had been a member of the St Louis Cardinals organisation in their farm system. Like so many others, he had applied to and been rejected by the USAAF cadet programme and had taken his business elsewhere, to the RCAF. He received pilot training and was assigned to the ferrying role, instead of a combat outfit as he had wanted. Like Don, Glover also rebelled at a role he loathed and thought up a way of getting out of it. He took off one day in an Airspeed Oxford transport plane and proceeded to power-dive it. The action resulted in sufficient, but not excessive, damage to the aircraft and Glover was hastily transferred to a combat outfit, the Fourth Fighter Group. His lust for air fighting was insatiable and he grew to be known in the group as a great natural pilot and an inspired Hun hunter.

Pierce McKennon (Mac) was a doctor's son and hailed from Fort Smith, Arkansas. Growing up, McKennon was dogged by two very different prospects, that of following in his father's footsteps to become a physician and inherit his father's practice, or to take the path his mother preferred for him, that of a concert pianist. To that end, she gave him a baby grand piano for his sixteenth birthday. He certainly demonstrated a powerful aptitude for the instrument, winning a music scholarship to the University of Arkansas. However, within a few weeks of arriving at the school, his classical tendencies were overwhelmed by an intense new love for swing and jazz – an affinity he would bring to Debden when he arrived via training in the RCAF.

Mac's other passions, apart from flying his Mustang, included a profound love of western novels and more than one 335th Fighter Squadron pilot remembered seeing him reading in the cockpit of his P-51 while overflying the Netherlands on a combat mission. Another favourite pursuit of this Arkansas traveller was hunting rabbits at night on the airfield using a jeep and a flashlight. But it was his piano playing, especially boogie, that made his fame in the officers' mess.

Eventually, Pierce McKennon rose to the rank of major and commanded the 335th Fighter Squadron. Among the best fighter pilots in the Fourth Fighter Group, he like most of them, had to overcome the tendency to go off hunting for the enemy on his own. It was a nasty habit that had to be curbed on the way to leadership and command responsibility. One of his pilots, a young lieutenant from California named George Green, also had a predilection for various transgressions. These included the unauthorised appropriation of a superior officer's jeep and other offences that frequently brought him to the attention of Mac for disciplinary action. Green, too, was a superb flier and an enthusiastic fighter who was always ready to tangle with the enemy.

By 18 March 1944, Mac's patience with young Green was wearing thin. The mission of the 335th Fighter Squadron on this day was a ground attack on the airfield at Prenzlau, forty miles from Berlin. It was known to be a hot flak area and after the strike, Mac ordered his charges to check their aircraft for damage. At that moment he noticed that his oil pressure gauge showed zero pressure. The flak had got him. His mind flashed back to the previous summer and the day he had been brought down in France by flak. He had been extraordinarily lucky then to evade capture and make his way safely back to Debden. He thought too of the time shortly after that incident, when he was hit again and slightly wounded, but was able to make it back to base, just.

This time, though, there was no question of making it back to Debden. He had nearly run out of time to do something to save himself and was rapidly running out of air as well. He made the decision and blew his canopy in preparation for baling out. But as he struggled to leave the crippled fighter, he realised that his G-suit was entangled and restraining him. He fought to free himself and escape the spinning Mustang.

George Green witnessed Mac's trouble and briefly thought about the group standing order prohibiting the attempted rescue of a fellow pilot, punishable by court martial if one succeeded, and by imprisonment in a German stalag if one failed. He watched as Mac floated safely to the ground some six miles from the Prenzlau airdrome they had attacked. He recalled another case in which an American fighter pilot had successfully carried out such a rescue. That guy had been flying a Thunderbolt, which had a larger cockpit than the Mustang.

Two dozen other pilots of the Fourth Fighter Group had observed Mac's parachute descent and landing, as they circled above him. Green worried about his CO's chances as he watched Mac run across the field where he had fallen, but he was buoyed by the protective presence of the other red-nosed Mustangs. He decided to land and pick up Mac.

Green made two passes over the field where Mac had landed, noting the direction in which the smoke from the burning wreck of Mac's Mustang was blowing. As Green completed the difficult approach and was nearly touching down, he spotted several German soldiers and a large Alsatian dog chasing Mac. He yelled into the R/T for his fellow pilots to strafe the Germans. A Mustang responded immediately, ending the threat to Mac. Now Green had to avoid hitting Mac's burning plane in the middle of the field. He used full flaps and prayed.

As soon as he brought his P-51 to a stop, he stood up and quickly began to shed his flying gear to make room in the cramped cockpit for Mac. Green climbed out onto the wing, getting rid of his parachute pack and dinghy and they both realised that there was now no possibility of either man baling out should they have to. Overhead, the other P-51s of the group continued to circle and give cover. As Mac was the taller and bigger of the two, it was quickly agreed that he would climb in and Green would sit on his lap and do the flying. Mac was crushed under the weight of Green and his feet were partially on the rudder pedals as there was nowhere else for them to be in the cramped space. Mac was, however, quietly happy to have yet another reprieve.

Bringing the canopy forward, George Green's leather-helmeted head now wedged against the Perspex. Both men knew that the take-off, if they managed it, would be rough on the bumpy meadow surface. Using the entire length of the field, Green gunned the big Packard-Merlin engine to full power, waited briefly and then released the brakes and the little fighter leapt ahead. At Debden, he would normally use about 900 yards of runway to lift his fully loaded Mustang into the air. Now he would have to get the bird airborne in less than 300 yards. The tall stand of trees rushed at them and when he had barely 80 mph, he pulled the stick back and forced the Mustang into the air. On the Debden runway, he would have waited until he had 150 mph. 'Goddamn, he made it,' came over the R/T from one of the circling P-51 pilots overhead.

'God, we're going to get home,' sighed Green, raising his wheels and Mac spoke to the circling pilots, 'Okay, fellas, form up and let's go home.' And to Green, he said: 'Oh, you crazy bastard.'

It took them two and a half hours, much of it over enemy-occupied territory, to make the trip back to Debden and Mac lost all feeling in his legs under the weight of Green. On the way, they encountered a dense haze and had to climb over it as Green was sitting too high to be able to fly the Mustang on instruments. They had to climb to nearly 18,000 feet and in the climb Mac, who had thrown away his oxygen mask with his other gear before they took off, lost consciousness. Green then took off his own oxygen mask and revived his CO. They took turns sucking oxygen until they were able to let down to a much lower altitude.

George Green called the Debden tower and requested permission to land. The reply came back: 'Is this an emergency?' 'I guess so,' said Green. 'We've got two pilots in this kite.'

A combat report of 1st Lt Pierce McKennon for 8 April 1944 describing one of his missions:

> I was flying Greenbelt White 3 when we tangled with 85 plus e/a heading towards the bombers. I cannot give a very coherent description because it's the first fight like it I have ever been in. Fw 190s were all over the place, and every time I turned around I started shooting. I made attacks on about five different Fw 190s; one of these I got strikes on. Looking over at one side of the fight there was an Fw 190 and a P-51 going round and round, neither getting deflection on the other. I dove towards the Fw 190 and clobbered him pretty good (about a 40-degree shot). He straightened out and I got in some more strikes on wing root and fuselage around the cockpit. He went into a sharp dive, and then I overshot him. I turned sharply. Looking down,

I saw him hit and litter a field with pieces. The fight started about 23,000 feet and finally ended up on the deck. Boy! It sure was a honey. I claim one Fw 190 Destroyed and one Damaged.

Another combat report – of 1st Lt Pierce McKennon, for 18 April 1944 read:

I was Caboose Blue 1, and we lost the Squadron in the clouds. Fifty to seventy-five Fw 190s attacked the bombers and came in under us. Several Huns stayed to attack the bombers. We went in, and I latched onto one that was beginning an attack. It was different from any I had seen before. The fuselage seemed longer and smaller from the cockpit forward. After several bursts, I finally hit him, knocking off a few pieces. He flicked and went into a dive with me following. He hit the deck at about a 45-degree angle and burned. Three Fw 190s then jumped me on the deck, but I outran them, climbed up, and came home.

The following account was given in a 24 December 1944 combat report of Lt George Green:

I was flying Caboose Blue 3 when I saw an Me 109 being chased by a P-47. I started after them with my Wingman following. As we closed, the P-47 broke away. I closed and fired. I observed strikes all over the e/a, and he flipped and spun out. That is all I saw of him. By the time I turned around, he had disappeared. I used the K-14 gunsight, which was very much to my advantage.

Canadian Jim Goodson had been a pantry boy on a Cunard liner after finishing high school in Toronto. He was in Paris when the Germans steamrolled through Poland, and he made his way to England where he booked a passage on the SS *Athenia*. While off the Hebrides, a German submarine torpedoed the *Athenia*. Goodson assisted the ship's medical personnel before making it to a lifeboat, which already contained some American college girls. Rescued by a Norwegian tanker, he tried again to return to Canada, this time as a steward aboard the motor vessel *Montrolite*. Once back in Canada, he joined the RCAF and ended up as an Eagle. At Debden, Goodson distinguished himself both as the third highest-scoring ace of the group, with fifteen air and fifteen ground kills. At age 23, Major Goodson was one of the leading lights of the famous Fourth Fighter Group.

In July 1944, the Fourth Fighter Group was briefed for a routine escort mission. Forming up over Saffron Walden, the group proceeded due east over Sudbury, Braintree, and Ipswich and headed out across the North Sea towards the Hook of Holland. They entered Germany north of Osnabruck and approached their rendezvous with the bomber force. Following the bombing, the group was relieved by another American fighter force that would take the bombers back to England. At that point the Fourth Fighter Group pilots were released to drop down and attack any enemy airfields that had not yet received their attention. As they descended, Jim Goodson spotted the airfield at Neu Brandenburg and a number of Bf 109s in the landing pattern, with several already on the ground. He focused on a Bf 109 that was about to land, blasting it with his guns. The Messerschmitt immediately ground-looped and burst into flames.

Pulling up and away from the drome, Goodson, known to his friends at Debden as 'Goody', noticed the stubby shape of an Me 163, the small rocket-powered fighter that the Germans had recently introduced into the air war. It was partially visible in a revetment on the perimeter of the field and he had to hold some height to attack it over the walls of the revetment. He continued the turn and aligned his Mustang on his target. Little orange fireballs of flak were rising towards him, seemingly slowly at first and then flashing past his plane. Just as he began firing on the Me 163, he felt the Mustang lurch and shudder and numbness in his right knee. He then felt the plane begin to stall and nursed it gently to the ground where it skidded to a halt.

Climbing out of the cockpit, Goodson noted the large amount of blood on his torn trouser leg. The rest of his squadron then passed slowly overhead and he signalled to them to shoot up and destroy his Mustang. He limped into the nearby woods, aware that he had brought the plane down only a few miles beyond the airfield he had just attacked. When he felt he had gone far enough to rest briefly, he inspected his wounds and found that the backs of his legs had been riddled with shrapnel. He removed the air map of Germany from one of his boots and discovered that he was roughly eighty miles from Rostock on the Baltic coast. With the help of the tiny compass in his escape kit and a lot of luck, he planned to walk there and then find a way to cross the Baltic to neutral Sweden. However, within two days he was picked up by some German soldiers after trying to cross a river.

Thereafter, he would come within moments of being shot, along with other prisoners in the jail where he was being held. Using his wit and imagination, he was able to persuade the prison *kommandant* to turn him over to the *Luftwaffe*. A *Luftwaffe* lieutenant and sergeant then arrived to escort him by train to Oberursel, the *Luftwaffe* interrogation centre near Frankfurt. They were to change trains in Berlin at the Friedrichstrasse Bahnhof and, on arriving there, were caught up in a massive American bombing raid. When they finally reached Oberursel, Goodson was interviewed at length by the renowned interrogator, Hanns Scharf, who already seemed to know more about the men and activities of the Fourth Fighter Group than Goodson. At Stalag Luft III in Silesia, Goodson was then reunited with several of his fellow pilots who had also been shot down and made prisoners-of-war.

When the Germans invaded Poland in September 1939, Winslow 'Mike' Sobanski was a student at the University of Warsaw. His reaction was to enlist in the Polish Air Force, but on applying he was told that there was no time to train him. He therefore joined the Polish Army as an infantryman and was on board a troop train *en route* to the Vistula front when the train was wrecked by German bombers. Badly wounded, Sobanski was put on another train, which took five days to arrive at a hospital, where he waited two additional days for treatment. He and other patients were soon captured by the Germans. However, as they believed he could not walk, they did not guard him and in the dark of night, he escaped.

Mike Sobanski had been born in the United States and, as an American citizen, was able to obtain a US visa. By the summer of 1940, he had managed to reach New York City. In one of the war's ironies, Sobanski lived in an apartment building that was also home to one James C. Cater. The two didn't meet then, but did four years later over Germany, Sobanski in a fighter of the Fourth Fighter Group and Cater in a bomber being escorted by the Debden pilots. An American news story about the raid appeared on the United Press wire and in it both men gave their US addresses as 400 East 57th Street, NYC.

Nick 'Cowboy' Megura came from Connecticut. The rebellious college student had been expelled from university and had been touring the United States in a Model A Ford when he took the opportunity to purchase a motorcycle. His mother decided the bike was dangerous and he would have to part with it. It led to his going to work for Vought-Sikorsky and learning to fly in his spare time. By September 1941, Nick was a flying instructor in the RAF when he had the chance to transfer into the USAAF, which is how he ended up in the Fourth Fighter Group at Debden. Fast-talking and frenetic, he was known for being excitable to the point of being almost incommunicative. He must have run his aeroplanes especially hard as his crew chief constantly had to replace the spark plugs in his aircraft. Later, Megura suffered the indignity of being shot down by a P-38 Lightning pilot who mistook Cowboy's Mustang for a Bf 109. Unable to free his jammed canopy, Megura could not bale out and somehow glided his plane to a landing in neutral Sweden. When he finally returned to Debden, he immediately chewed out his engineering officer over the canopy that wouldn't jettison.

The following account was given in a 4 March 1944 combat report of 1st Lt Nick Megura:

I was flying Pectin Blue 1 when we R/Vd with the Combat Wing of B-17s west of Berlin. As we positioned ourselves ahead of the bombers, we saw many single and double smoke trails coming from all directions – at our level and above. Fifteen plus Me 109s and Fw 190s made a frontal attack on the bombers and were driven down. We gave chase from 27,000 to 22,000 feet and up again along side the bombers. I investigated eight plus a/c, which I identified as Fw 190s. They were going away from the bombers. I was unable to close after chasing from 27,000 to 5,000 feet. I found myself alone, and I took a good look around. At 12,000 feet I noticed three Me 109s very close at 8 o'clock. I easily outclimbed them and reached 31,000 feet about 25 miles behind the bombers. Seeing two smoke trails at 9 o'clock, I bounced the nearest. It turned out to be a P-51 ('WD'-335 Squadron). The other a/c was a white-nosed Me 109. I joined the P-51, and I gave chase to the e/a as it half-rolled into a vertical dive. I followed the P-51, 'WD' Squadron, clocking 550 IAS. At 18,000 feet the P-51's port wing came off at the root and disintegrated. The canopy and tail came off as I dodged past. Pieces carried away my antennae and hit my stabiliser.

My controls were frozen, and I had to use trim to pick up the nose. This brought me behind the e/a, but I was overshooting. The canopy frosted on the inside, but disappeared when I opened the window. The only evasive action taken by the e/a was a weave to right or left. I barrel-rolled and positioned myself 1,000 feet above and to the side of him. I dropped flaps and dove astern. This engagement brought us down to 2,000 feet. Just as I was about to fire, the e/a pulled up sharply to 3,000 feet, and jettisoned its canopy. The pilot baled out. The e/a crashed and burned. The pilot landed 50 feet from the wreckage. I cleared my tail and saw that I was right over a grass A/D [aerodrome]. Directly ahead of me was a large hangar with a Ju 52 parked alongside. I pushed everything to the firewall and hit the deck. I opened up on the Ju 52, observing only one gun firing. Shooting low, I brought my fire into the e/a itself and noticed flames leaping out as I hopped over the hangar and hit the deck weaving. A few miles away, I saw a locomotive pulling 10 or 12 cars. I pulled up to 50 feet, looked back at the A/D, and saw black smoke rising behind the hangar. I opened fire on the engine and noticed strikes. The train came to a halt. Seeing that it was time to 'leave out', I set course for home.

The 6 March 1944 mission was described in the combat report of 1st Lt Nick Megura:

As a spare, I saw no vacancy in Pectin Squadron, so I filled in with 335 Squadron as White 2. We R/Vd south of Berlin and positioned ourselves on the lead box. We saw twelve plus smoke trails coming from 12 o'clock and high, 30 miles ahead. 'Upper' positioned the Group up-sun, below condensation height, and waited. The trails finally converged at 9 o'clock to the bombers and started to close on them. Six thousand feet below the trails were 20 plus S/E [single-engine] e/a, line abreast, sweeping the area for 20 plus T/E [twin-engine] rocket-carrying a/c. 'Upper' led the Group head-on into the front wave of e/a. I passed over on top and started after three Me 110s. They split and headed for the deck without firing their rockets. I started to follow, but I took a good look around and noticed some Me 110s of the cover coming down.

I broke into an a/c closing from 8 o'clock, but identified it as a P-51. I jumped three others, which were Me 110s, just as they let go their rockets, which burst behind the last bombers. I raked the three Me 110s, which were flying wing tip to wing tip. As the number 1 e/a broke into me, I saw strikes all over his cockpit and both engines as he disappeared under me. I cleared my tail and saw a P-51 covering me 500 yards behind and to the side. I closed on the Me 110 and fired. I saw strikes with pieces falling off, and I saw an explosion in the cockpit. I pulled up over him and saw him go into a vertical dive, pouring out black smoke. I climbed starboard toward an Me 110 who was climbing up behind the bombers. The e/a started violent evasive action toward the deck. There I closed on him with one working gun. He led me over an A/D. I saw strikes on his port engine and cockpit. I pulled aside, overshot, and closed firing. The e/a was hugging the deck as I got hits on his wing and cockpit. His port wing tore off as the e/a hit the ground and nosed over. I got away fast and pulled up behind an Fw 190 carrying a belly tank. I pressed the teat and nothing happened. I closed fast and pulled up to keep from ramming him. I hit the deck; tried my guns on a train, again with no results; and came home.

There was always a concern among many fighter leaders in the ETO that if a pilot got married, he would become overly cautious and his aggressiveness and value to the group as a fighter pilot would be reduced. Willard 'Millie' Millikan was one of the older boys in the outfit. At 26, he was not what some called a natural. Millikan, like Blakeslee's predecessor, Colonel Chesley Peterson, had been washed out of the same flying school at San Diego. Like so many of the others at Debden, Millie had made it to the big show via the RCAF, where his instructor had urged him to forget about flying fighters in combat and go for an assignment ferrying aircraft. But Millie persevered and eventually became an exceptional fighter pilot. He also met and married an English girl and they had a daughter. He never did become cautious or lose his edge.

Lieutenant Ralph Hofer was known as 'the Kid' to everyone at the Fourth Fighter Group. He had come from Salem in Missouri, where he had excelled as a boxer in the light-heavyweight division of the Golden Gloves tournament of 1940. A superb athlete, Hofer had also played some football before crossing the Canadian border to join the RCAF. He had absolutely no interest in aeroplanes or flying, but was infected by the enthusiasm of the many young Americans he met there and was happy to follow their lead into aviation cadet training. While in his cadet uniform, he happened to be spotted in Chicago one day by an advertising man who offered him $50 to appear in some photographs that would be used in billboards for Coca Cola. The advertisements were to appear over the next few years, but Hofer would never see them for he would be in England fighting with the men of the Fourth Fighter Group. The Kid always had a smile on his face and invariably wore his blue football jersey with the orange number 78 on it. With longish chestnut hair, he was a unique and colourful sight around the Debden base.

Most fighter pilots didn't even see an enemy fighter, much less shoot one down, until they had flown eight or ten missions. Hofer located a Focke-Wulf 190, the pride of the *Luftwaffe*, during his very first mission and shot it down, to the amazement of his fellow pilots. He followed the kill by diving down and shooting up a German flak boat in the English Channel. In short order, the Kid was an ace, having amassed the required five kills. Never shy about the prey he sought, Hofer is well remembered for the time he had closed on a German fighter and was blasting away at the victim when, with no warning, his engine quit. He had forgotten to switch to his wing tanks when his fuselage tank had run dry. Seeing this, another Fourth Fighter Group pilot insinuated himself into the action and opened fire on Hofer's target. Thinking quickly, the Kid shouted over the R/T: 'Break! Break!' Believing a German fighter to be on his tail, the opportunistic Mustang pilot broke off sharply to his left, leaving Hofer to resume his attack.

The concept of team play had been uppermost in the RAF, and later the USAAF, training of the Debden pilots and Hofer was gaining a reputation as an undisciplined loner. Jim Clark, his squadron commanding officer, was a patient man, but in time his patience was beginning to wear thin. Jim Goodson recalled:

Hofer had had to turn back from a mission because one of his droppable tanks wasn't feeding through. The Kid screamed back to base, landed in a steep turn and sped over to the revetment where his faithful Alsatian dog, Duke, and his capable crew chief were waiting. The mechanics quickly fixed the block in the fuel system, and Hofer immediately took off again. But it was too late to catch the main mission, so he simply flew his own separate show, scouring Belgium and France for German aircraft. Not finding any, he did a little ground strafing on his way out over Holland. He dodged the flak coming out over the coast, but the real flak was waiting for him when he got back to base at Debden. Not only his squadron commander, but the commanding officer of the group, Don Blakeslee, were waiting for him.

That evening, Don, Jim, 'Gunner' Halsey, 'Deacon' Hively and I were discussing the problem of Ralph Hofer. Someone wanted him busted, someone suggested the toughest punishment would be a transfer to another outfit, and someone said the problem would soon handle itself. If the Kid continued to goof off on his own, one day he wouldn't come back.

When Blakeslee asked my opinion, I thought awhile before answering: 'First, as far as Hofer is concerned, I don't see him as plotting to break out of formation, just to build up his score. His reaction is as spontaneous and uncontrollable as that Alsatian pup of his when he throws a stick for him. But what we're really talking about is the old argument of flight defensive discipline versus individual aggressive attack. The team approach versus the Prima Donna.' The average age of our foursome must have been about twenty-three, but they solemnly nodded when I went on: 'We had flying discipline drilled into us in the early RAF days, and the worst imaginable sin was to go off on your own or attack before ordered to; but we were fighting a defensive war then, and everyone from Air Marshal Dowding on down knew that if we didn't conserve our outnumbered planes and pilots, we'd probably lose the damned war. But the Battle of Britain is over now, and the Battle of Germany is starting. We're now on the offensive and they are on the defensive. We've got the planes with the range and performance to do it, so we better use them. After all, a fighter pilot is either the hunter or the hunted, and, if he's the hunted, he's in trouble. I'd hate to think there was no place in this outfit for guys like Hofer, even if they are wild. The thing is to control them without killing their spirit. The spirit of the outfit is the spirit of the people in it, and we need all of that we can get. You'll always have plenty of good pilots to keep the squadron going as a fighting force – offensive and defensive, but let's find a way to keep the wild ones with us.'

A combat report of Lt. Ralph K. Hofer for 18 March 1944 had the following account:

As we dove, I saw a good bounce on an Me 109 and dropped W/T [wing tanks] and went after him. I saw strikes and an explosion as pieces flew off and black smoke poured out of the falling e/a. I saw an A/D with a four-engine a/c that looked like a Liberator. I fired on an Me 109, which went into the clouds but popped out again as the canopy came off. The pilot baled out. Major Goodson confirmed this a/c.

I bounced another 109 but lost him in the clouds. I set course for the target, and I saw two 109s in front and above me. I climbed to attack them. At about 600 yards, my prop ran away, and I lost flying speed. I was recording a terrific amount of boost and rpm, so I set course for Switzerland. As I passed into Switzerland, I started to climb to bale out, and my prop came back to normal. I decided that with a little luck I could make it back home. On the way, I saw three 109s shoot down a Mustang before I could help. I landed at Manston with six gallons of gas.

This combat report of Lt. Ralph K. Hofer described another mission:

I was flying Pectin Purple 1 when we R/Vd with bombers at 1150 hours, south of Koblenz. We intercepted and chased 15 plus e/a that attacked bombers from 1 o'clock. I saw Lt Wynn fire on an Me 109; the pilot baled out. In positioning myself on four Fw 190s, I was bounced by four e/a from above. I dropped wing tanks, broke sharply port and evaded. I positioned for a bounce on one e/a, and I was in turn bounced by two e/a. I evaded sharply down into a cloud and continued to chase the first e/a. I climbed back on top, hoping to find him there. I again broke down through cloud, where I observed two Me 109s to my port. I dodged up for a while and then went to the deck. I fired on a locomotive and observed many strikes. I tested my guns on a power pylon and a control tower near Koblenz.

Another combat report of Lt Ralph K. Hofer for 24 May 1944 gave the following account:

I was Flying Cobweb White 3 and had rendezvoused with bombers when 30 plus bandits at 35,000 feet were sighted coming in at 12 o'clock to us. We had climbed up to 30,000 feet when I sighted four Me 109s coming in below us. I attacked, but lost sight of them in the haze. I pulled up and sighted three FW 190s attacking a B-17 that was returning. We bounced them, and I started shooting. We were trying to scare them off, but they didn't seem to see me. Finally I closed on one, getting strikes. The aircraft started smoking, the hood was jettisoned, and the pilot baled. The other two broke up to the left.

I then pulled up and saw Lt Fraser, my wingman, behind the other two Fw 190s. One of them made a split 'S', with Lt Fraser following. He did a split 'S', and I followed at 14,000 feet. I got a few scattered hits. At 10,000 feet, below the clouds, I got more strikes in a tight turn. He pulled sharply up into a cloud and jettisoned his hood. I did not see the pilot bale out, but the a/c crashed in a field burning. Its ammo exploded in intervals. I took a picture of this.

Jim Clark was deputy group commander to Don Blakeslee and came from celebrated stock. Aged 24, Lieutenant-Colonel Clark was the rock-solid, steady number two that every group commander needed and could be relied on to lead the group on missions with competence and efficiency. His uncle, Tommy Hitchcock, had been a famous polo player and a member of the Lafayette Escadrille of the First World War. In his time at Debden, Clark met and married the daughter of an English earl. Oddly, he is also known to have argued against his own promotion to the rank of captain and his award of the Distinguished Flying Cross.

The combat report of Major James Clark for 8 March 1944 had the following description:

We attacked five 109s from below. I followed one down to 8,000 feet where I fired three short bursts. I observed a few strikes in the cockpit area. The e/a flicked and dove straight into the ground. I claim one 109 Destroyed.

Duane Beeson of Boise, Idaho, was the other half of a long-standing, on-going competition with Don Gentile to be the top-scoring pilot of the Fourth Fighter Group. Their friendly rivalry had been instrumental in motivating the other pilots to achieve more kills on the way to making the Fourth Fighter Group the highest scoring fighter group in the ETO. Small of frame, with a strident voice, the fastidious Bee epitomised the eager, aggressive fighter pilot type of his era. Beeson paid great attention to detail, one of many reasons for his success with the group. He had intended to become a lawyer until the war came along. He got into the RAF and, for whatever reason, emerged from training with an exceptionally powerful need to kill Germans . . . as many and as soon as possible. By the end of his days with the group, Bee had been credited with eighteen aerial kills and seven enemy aircraft destroyed on the ground.

A student of aviation history and the legendary fighter pilots past and present, Major Beeson worked hard at improving his aerial gunnery skill. He even adopted the practice of the great Adolf 'Sailor' Malan, the RAF Battle of Britain ace credited with thirty-two kills. He would brace his elbows against the sides of the cockpit, holding the stick with both hands and pressing the firing button with his left thumb. The boyish-looking Bee soon had a reputation as a deadly hunter. Seemingly fearless, his gun-camera film invariably showed huge pieces flying off the aircraft of his victim, or oil from the damaged German plane fogging his camera lens, so near did he close on the enemy in his zeal for the kill.

The combat report of (then) Captain D. W. Beeson for 5 March 1944 described the following mission:

> I was flying as Pectin Green Leader. Col Blakeslee was forced to abort due to engine trouble. This left me leading the Squadron. The bombers turned back about 60 miles south of Bordeaux. Just after they had completed their turn, they were attacked by about six Me 109s. I sighted two e/a who had just gone through one box [formation] of bombers and were turning to go through another. Our Section immediately dove toward them. They saw us coming and whipped into a tight turn. I took a head-on shot at them, then pulled up above for another pass. They again turned into us, and I took another head-on shot and pulled up again. There were now several other Mustangs around who were trying to get these Me 109s. As the e/a went over into a dive, the Mustangs went after them. I had managed to keep my speed pretty high and was able to get on the tail of one. We broke up their line astern formation. Before I opened fire, I saw Lt Pisanos getting very good strikes on his e/a. I had evidently struck my 109 in one of the head-on attacks, for he was already smoking slightly. After opening fire at about 150 yards and getting more strikes, he began to smoke quite badly. As I overshot the e/a, the pilot baled out. I began an orbit and called for the other Mustangs to rejoin.

We were now at about 7,000 feet, so we climbed up to 12,000 feet. We flew near Bordeaux and saw Fw 200s, an He 111, and other a/c sitting on an aerodrome. As we had already awakened the flak gunners, it would have been foolish to attack after flying over. So, we flew on. Shortly afterwards, we sighted an aerodrome about 60 miles north of Bordeaux. We dove to the deck and approached at about 400 mph. I opened fire on an Fw 200 and saw strikes around the engines. We headed across the aerodrome with a little flak bursting around us. As I reached the other side, I felt a heavy blow on the a/c and was thrown over on my side. I had great difficulty regaining control. The rudders were very stiff, and I was forced to hold hard left rudder all the way back to base. I had been hit by flak, which left a large hole in my rudder.

About five minutes after our attack, Captain Peterson shot down an Fw 200, which I confirmed. He and Lt Carr joined me as we came out. Three hours later, we landed at our base. I also confirmed one Me 109 shot down by Lt Pisanos. I claimed one Me 109 Destroyed and one Fw 200 Damaged. This claim was confirmed in writing by Captain Kenneth D. Peterson of 336 Squadron.

The combat report of Captain Duane Beeson for 23 March 1944 gave the following account:

As we approached the bombers, there were many e/a around. One Me 109 made a head-on pass through our Squadron. He then circled to come at us again, so I turned after him. He dove, and as I closed, he pulled up into a steep climb. I followed; closed; and got good strikes on him. He began to smoke and headed for the clouds. I followed and clobbered him again as he came out of the clouds. He stuck with his plane and crash-landed in a field where I strafed him. His engine began to flame as the pilot got out of the cockpit and ran across the field. He fell behind a fence post as I made another pass.

I made a pass at a freight train and got good strikes on the engine. I then climbed after an Me 109 with its wheels down, but he went into a cloud just as I saw tracers going past my port wing. I quickly broke to starboard and saw an Me 109 behind me. He pulled into a cloud from where he again dove, but I was able to get on his tail and saw many flashes as I fired.

He jettisoned his hood, but I kept firing. Oil from the e/a covered my windscreen. He baled out, but his 'chute did not open. His plane crashed nearby and burst into flames.

Raised on a farm in south-eastern Pennsylvania, Frank Speer graduated from Allentown High School in 1939. He married his high school sweetheart in the month before the Japanese attacked Pearl Harbor. Being patriotic and anxious to fly in the coming war, Frank enlisted in the US Army Air Corps, emerging from the aviation cadet programme in 1943.

The combat report of Lt Frank Speer for 24 May 1944 gave the following account:

> We sighted about 20 Me 109s and Fw 190s at 30,000 feet, 12 o'clock to the bombers and 5,000 feet above us. I was flying Green 3, and our target was six Me 109s, which were in a gentle turn to the left. We climbed and joined their orbit. We got fairly close to them and started firing before they broke. Only the two we fired on broke. I got strikes on the first burst, and the e/a split Sd with me on his tail. He went straight down skidding, rolling, and he took violent evasive action. I kept firing short bursts. Pieces were coming off him all the time, two of which damaged my plane slightly. We went through some contrails. I was directly above him going straight down when he seemed to hit compressibility. His plane was shuddering violently. I had to put down 20 degrees of flaps to keep from overrunning him. I was indicating above 500 mph. The e/a started to pull out, and doing the same, I blacked out. When I came to, he was diving again, and I saw his canopy come off as he bailed out. The kite was last seen going straight down at about 9,000 feet, doing at least 500 mph.

The 9 May 1944 combat report of Lt Frank Speer gave the following account:

> Flying line abreast in number 3 position to Lt Blanchfield, we dove at 1,000 hours onto the airfield. We came over the field in a dive from 200 feet down. I believe Lt Blanchfield was shooting at a flak tower, as was his number 2. I was shooting at hangars and buildings and I didn't see Lt Blanchfield get hit. As we passed the field, I saw his plane streaming white smoke as he pulled up to about 3,000 feet, very slowly, on a course of 240 degrees from the field. His jacket was covered with oil, which also covered the side of the plane. He seemed to have lost both his oil and glycol, and the engine was detonating violently.
>
> Blanchfield climbed out of the cockpit as the plane rolled in a half roll to the left. His radio seemed to have been shot out, also, but he was using both hands and making signs. He seemed to be unhurt. When he left the plane, it was going about 150 mph, and his 'chute

opened almost immediately. He landed in a small wood. We didn't stay around to see him get out because he was near a small town, and we didn't want to attract attention to him.

His plane immediately burst into flames and burned furiously about half a mile from where he landed.

Lt Frank Speer also recalled:

Looking out of our Dispersal window today, we saw a very good example of Anglo-American co-operation. A farmer was gathering up his bundles of wheat, assisted by a number of crew chiefs, assistant crew chiefs, and armourers who had finished a hard days' work on their planes. The weather looked a little uncertain, so their help was doubly welcome.

Howard 'Deacon' Hively had accumulated many flying hours while chauffeuring his college geology professor around the state of Oklahoma as the professor took aerial photos of the terrain. With the coming of war in Europe, Deacon noticed a poster inviting Americans to join the RAF's Eagle Squadron. He showed his logbook to the recruiters and was soon training at Bakersfield, California. He arrived in England on 1 September 1941 and, after a clerical error involved him in a commando course, he was soon back on flying duties. He finished up at Debden with twelve aerial victories and three ground kills. The combat report of 1st Lt H. D. Hively for 5 March 1944 gave the following account:

I was leading Pectin Red Section south of Bordeaux, near the rear of the bombers at 15,000 feet. When e/a were reported coming through the formation, I turned port and followed Pectin Leader in an attack on two Me 109s. I could not break into the queue because there were about six P-51s after these two. I was circling above the fight, and I was waiting for a chance to break in when I noticed four e/a approaching from the south at about 8,000 feet.

I turned toward them and identified them as Me 109s. I attacked from their 9 o'clock. They broke into me, and we went around and around in a port-climbing orbit. At about 13,000 feet I started getting deflection. Two of the e/a broke starboard out of the turn and started for the deck. I picked up my flaps, turned and chased. For a second it looked as if I wasn't closing, so I took two short bursts at about 800 yards just for meanness. I noticed I was closing rapidly. I chopped everything, let down my flaps (20 degrees), and closed to about 50 yards on the number two e/a. He turned starboard as I fired, and I observed many strikes on the bottom and the top-side of the fuselage and the wing root. When I closed my throttle, I screwed my trim so that I started sliding out to the left. As I slid by, I saw his starboard wing crumple about two feet from the wing root. I then slid right on the number one e/a and fired. I observed five or six good hits on his fuselage, underside, and just back of the cockpit. I slid on past to his port, picked up my flaps, and followed him down in a gentle diving turn from 3,000 feet. He never pulled out. The e/a went in with a large column of dust and black smoke. Neither pilot baled out.

The Me 109s were a dirty-green colour with bright orange spinners. It was also my observation that [the] P-51 can out turn, out climb, out dive, and out run Me 109s at those altitudes, especially above 12,000 feet. Also, I would like to caution those concerned to go easy on the trim in these airplanes, because it really takes hold at high speeds.

Like so many of his fellow Fourth Fighter Group pilots, Donald Emerson was a child of the Great Depression years, growing up in the farmlands of North Dakota and Minnesota. An ace with seven enemy aircraft destroyed, Captain Emerson had flown nearly one hundred missions by Christmas Day 1944. It was during the Battle of the Bulge, and Emerson had become separated from the other aircraft of the group. He was engaged in combat with six Fw 190s and, despite the odds, managed to shoot down two of the German fighters before exhausting his ammunition. He then ducked into some nearby clouds. While crossing into Allied territory, his Mustang was hit by ground fire and crash-landed near the Holland-Belgium border, killing the twenty-one-year-old pilot.

The following is an extract from a letter written on 9 April 1944 by Emerson to his family:

One of these days you will be reading about a new fighter ace who just lately boosted his score to a record high of 30 German planes destroyed. He is Capt. Don Gentile and I'm proud to be flying in the same squadron with him. He had 14 to his credit when I came here and has really been going to town lately. The news-reel cameramen have been here all day taking pictures of him. I am sending a clipping taken from a London paper telling about a little expedition we went on the other day. This Gentile got five Jerry planes that day. I was flying with him and didn't do so bad myself. I destroyed two and damaged a couple others. Our squadron hit this airdrome and left just about every plane on it in flames. Incidentally a plane destroyed on the ground counts as much as one in the air. Altogether I have three to my credit now.

In a letter dated 31 October 1942 Emerson wrote:

I admit I'm sticking my neck out but I'd rather take my chances in the air than in the infantry, armoured division, tank corps or the navy. Of course it's dangerous but name me a war job that isn't. Anyway I'm one of those that believe that if a guy is supposed to lose his life in this war it will happen no matter what or where and vice versa.

The combat report of Lt Donald Emerson had the following account:

I was leading Becky Blue Section when two bogies passed under us from 9 o'clock. As soon as we determined that they were bandits, we turned hard to starboard and opened up. The Me 410s headed for the bombers. Col Blakeslee's Section chased them line astern. They turned starboard, and my section dropped tanks and cut them off. One of the 410s split Sd for the deck, and I continued after the other. I closed rapidly taking several deflection shots and then closed line astern. I got several strikes, which set his starboard engine on fire. I then pulled up to one side expecting him to explode or go into the deck as he was in a steep spiral. At that time, Lt Netting made several passes at the Me 410 and watched it crash-land. Lt Netting had also made a pass at the 410 before I set it on fire. We formed-up and made a pass on several Seaplanes on a lake, but I had only one gun operating. I don't think I did much damage to the Do-18. I claim one Me 410 Destroyed, shared with Lt Netting, and one Do-18 Damaged.

The combat report of Lt Donald Emerson for 2 July 1944 also described the following mission:

I was leading a Section of six 336 Fighter Squadron pilots. We were flying north from the target after a group of Me 109s that had been reported at the base of the clouds. I sighted an Me 109 flying with some Mustangs as if he were part of their Section. I pulled in line astern of him and gave chase, but closed very slowly as my engine would not pull more than 40″ of Mercury (without my knowledge, the air intake was set in unrammed filtered air).

When I finally got within reasonable range, Lt Higgins was also in position to fire. I got numerous strikes on the fuselage and cockpit of the 109, which then pulled up in a steep climb. I stalled out and started to spin. When I recovered, the Me 109 was spiralling down. I followed him down because I was not sure if he was out of control or not. At this time, I saw pieces of the wing come off, and the 109 continued to spiral into the deck. I saw no one bale out of the e/a. I claim one Me 109 Destroyed, shared with Lt Higgins.

Louis 'Red Dog' Norley served with all three squadrons of the Fourth Fighter Group and by VE Day had led the 334th and 335th Squadrons as their commander. At the start of his third tour of duty, Norley had accrued more than 550 hours of combat flying. By the war's end he had been credited with 16.33 enemy aircraft destroyed. Norley was also indirectly involved in the bizarre events of 18 March, when George Green landed his Mustang in a German meadow to stage the dramatic piggyback rescue of his squadron leader, Pierce McKennon (Mac). On an earlier mission, Green had been flying number two to Norley. They were about to bounce two Bf 109s and Norley ordered Green to stay with him and give him cover while they made the attack. Norley shot down one of the German fighters and looked around for Green. He soon spotted his wingman far below near the cloud tops, having left him to go after the second Bf 109. At that moment, the German pilot had position advantage on Green and was about to attack the American, who was only saved by Norley's superb flying skills and experience. Following that mission, Norley wanted Mac to transfer Green out of the squadron. Mac was inclined to agree, but decided instead to give Green one more chance. Then came the famous rescue of Mac by Green. Later, when asked why he had done it, Green had replied, 'I figured I owed the guy a favour'.

The 17 September 1944 combat report of Captain Louis H. Norley gave the following account of a mission:

I was leading Caboose Squadron when Caboose Blue Section was bounced by 15 plus e/a from 6 o'clock high. Caboose Blue 3 called for a break, but it was too late for one of the Sections, either 2 or 4 was already going down in flames. The bandits had been flying at the base of a layer of haze and with their light grey color were very difficult to see.

I dropped my tanks. In a port break, I met an a/c head-on firing at me. These were supposedly Me 109s, and this one, with an in-line engine, looked like an e/a. I fired a short burst at long range. I then noticed two Fw 190s on his tail, the closest one firing, and getting strikes as it became apparent that the plane I fired on was a P-51. I broke up, coming down on the tail of the Fw 190 as he broke off his attack and turned to port. I dropped 20 degrees of flaps and turned with him, the other 190 being attacked by my wingman. I fired. The 190 rolled and started to split-S, but levelled out and started to climb.

I fired again with no results. He levelled off and did some skidding evasion efforts as I closed, firing and skidding past him. He dove to port, allowing me to drop back on his tail. I fired, getting many strikes on his wings and fuselage. He flicked over on his back. The canopy and some pieces flew off, and he went into a vertical dive, crashing into a farm yard where the plane blew up. I climbed up, found my wingman, assembled the Squadron over Wesel, and completed our mission.

From the diary of Lt Jack Raphael, 336th Fighter Squadron:

26 January 1944 – Started out as Red 2 to do a dry-run dive bombing. Cloud from 8,000 on up. Got in White section's slipstream at 19,000 and spun out, recovering on instruments at 9,000. Shaky do to say the least. Got a new pilot named Skilton. He was the first American-trained type to join the squadron. Wrote several letters and turned in rather early.

CHAPTER SEVEN

Mustangs

From the diary of 1st Lt Jack Raphael, 336th Fighter Squadron:

14 February 1944 – Did a short air test on VF-M. Had planned a longer one, but the visibility was very poor and I couldn't do it. Got our first Mustang going. Some of the fellows checked out in it. George and I caught the early train to London. Got a room in the Jules Club and then went over to Marselle's for a while. Ate at the Criterion and then went to the Studio Club. Left there about 10:30 pm and called it a night.

In the late 1930s, the British Air Ministry believed that the Vickers-Supermarine Spitfire and the Hawker Hurricane (both Rolls-Royce Merlin-powered fighters) met the RAF Fighter Command requirement for the defence of Great Britain. The Air Ministry had no particular interest in any other fighter types and certainly none in anything being produced in the United States. There was simply no match for the speed, manoeuvrability and firepower of the Spitfire at that time. However, the Spitfire was rather short on range and, as the European war entered its fifth month, it became clear that the RAF needed a fighter of much greater range, in order to meet the growing Italian threat to Egypt and that of the Japanese to Singapore. The Air Ministry decided that it needed 1,000 new fighters for delivery in 1941 and frantically placed an order with the Brewster Airplane Company in the US for its Buffalo. Brewster, however, could supply no more than 170 Buffalos during 1941, and the Air Ministry had to look elsewhere.

By the end of 1939, France too needed new fighters and agreed with the Curtiss Company of New York on the purchase of 420 Hawk H75A and 259 H81A fighters, an export version of the US Army Air Corps P-40. The French were hoping that by 1941 the US Army would allow them to buy P-38s and P-39s, the aircraft they really wanted.

Soon, a joint Anglo-French Purchasing Commission (AFPC) was formed. After many complex and frustrating negotiations with the American aircraft manufacturers (Republic, Bell, and Lockheed, in addition to Curtiss), the Commission finally elected to order 667 export models of the Lockheed Model 322 (a P-38 variant). This was despite the fact that it could not be delivered in quantity until late 1941.

In June 1940, after France had fallen to the Germans, the RAF inherited the Curtiss aircraft ordered by the French, and came to regret the AFPC commitment to the Lockheed 322. In late May, Curtiss changed its production plans and offered the P-40D, which both the US Army Air Corps and the RAF believed was a better aircraft than anything else then available. It also had an earlier delivery date. The RAF quickly bought 471 of one version and 560 of a second, naming them Tomahawk and Kittyhawk.

The British, however, still had a pressing fighter requirement. The RAF needed more fighters than Curtiss alone could build and, even before the Kittyhawk production programme had begun, went shopping for another source of P-40 production. On 25 February 1940, the RAF approached North American Aviation based in Los Angeles, whose Harvard trainer had served them impressively since 1938. The company's president, J. H. 'Dutch' Kindelberger, was asked to consider building P-40s for the RAF.

Kindelberger's chief designer was a 40-year-old German engineer named Edgar Schmued. He had emigrated first to Brazil and then to the United States in 1930, and had worked for North American since February 1936. His colleagues regarded him as a quiet, friendly, methodical man with a burning ambition to design the best fighter plane in the world. He had been working on design ideas for several months, using a German engineering handbook, together with his own personal notebook of technical formulae.

Rumours that the British wanted North American to build P-40s for them had been circulating in the Los Angeles (Inglewood) factory and Schmued was well prepared when Dutch Kindelberger dropped by his office one afternoon in early March. He asked the designer, 'Ed, do we want to build P-40s here?' Schmued responded, 'Well, Dutch, don't let us build an obsolete airplane. Let's build a new one. We can design and build a better one.' Kindelberger replied, 'Ed, I'm going to England in about two weeks and I need an inboard profile, three-view drawing, performance estimate, specifications and some detail drawings on the gun installations to take along. Then I would like to sell that new model airplane that you develop.' He told the designer to make it the fastest plane he could, and to 'build it around a man that is five feet ten inches tall and weighs 140 pounds'. He said that it should have two 20 mm cannon in each wing and should meet all the design requirements of the US Army Air Corps. With that, North American Specification NAA SC1050 was issued and work on the new fighter began on 15 March 1940.

Armed with the papers he had requested, Kindelberger left for Britain later that month as Ed Schmued and his design team started building a paper and plaster-of-Paris mock-up of the new aircraft. On Thursday 11 April, Sir Henry Self, director of the AFPC, signed a letter of intent to purchase 400 Model NA-50B, NAA Spec 1592 fighters. The greatest fighter aircraft of the war had been launched.

The Lend-Lease programme had not yet begun and Britain wanted to keep its costs down on the new aircraft, which was to be powered by an Allison engine. The $40,000 agreed unit price for the aircraft was not to be exceeded by the manufacturer, who also undertook to deliver 320 aircraft between January and the end of September 1941, and fifty per month thereafter. It was estimated that the actual cost to Britain would be $37,590 per plane.

By merging his earlier fighter design concepts and a new laminar flow aerofoil, Schmued shaped the newly designated Model NA-73. Final official British approval was given on 20 July, after the fall of France and the start of the Battle of Britain.

The design assignment was apportioned to several specialised groups under Schmued's supervision. He estimated that a hundred days would be needed to build the first experimental aeroplane. The British wanted the aircraft to be flight-tested, de-bugged and in production within one year. Within the company there were many concerns about the new wing and how it might perform. Exhaustive testing proved its viability, and brilliant scheduling and co-ordination resulted in the first aircraft being completed by both engineering and the workshop in just 102 days. In 1984, Schmued reflected:

> We could never build another plane today in a hundred days. Today they just don't have what it takes. There are too many levels of authority within the building companies. They have a president, a vice-president and many other levels. We had formed an exceptional group of engineers. There was an enthusiasm in this group that was unequalled anywhere. We worked every day until midnight. On Sundays we quit at 6 pm, so we knew we had a weekend.

Unfortunately, the Allison people at their plant in Indianapolis failed to deliver the engine for the new fighter test plane and it was a further eighteen days before it arrived for installation in the airframe. The

Flight Test Division of North American then prepared the necessary instrumentation and, on 11 October 1940, the aircraft was given its initial engine run-up tests.

Initial flight-testing began on Saturday 26 October, and continued until 20 November. That day the test pilot neglected to put the fuel valve on 'reserve', and ran out of fuel after fifteen minutes of flight. He was forced to put the precious prototype down on a freshly ploughed field and as he landed, the wheels dug into the soft ground, causing the aircraft to flip onto its back. The pilot was uninjured, but the aircraft was badly damaged, requiring a time-consuming rebuild. Schmued's team decided to have the second aeroplane on the shop line (actually scheduled to be the first production aircraft) prepared for flight test, so as not to delay the gathering of the critical test data, which was needed immediately if the new aircraft was to be produced on time.

Even before the NA-73 was flown for the first time, the British had ordered a further 300 aircraft, making a new total of 620. A letter from the British purchasing authority to North American dated 9 December referred to the fighter as Mustang, its new official name. In August 1941, the first Mustang 1 to be accepted for delivery to the British was crated and shipped via the Panama Canal, from Long Beach, California, to England, where it was assembled and test-flown on 11 November. During August and September 1941, the US Army also accepted several of the new aircraft, and designated the first of them XP-51. It was flown to Wright Field in Ohio for additional testing and evaluation, while the North American Flight Test Division continued to test two examples at the California facility.

All 620 aircraft of the British order were completed and delivered by July 1942, and Mustang 1s were in service with fifteen RAF Army Co-operation squadrons by December. They were used primarily for reconnaissance on low-level cross-Channel dashes, in which they also shot up German trains, barges and troop concentrations, as well as performing valuable photo reconnaissance work. The RAF pilots flying these Mustang 1s liked them and thought they were easily the best American fighters to have reached Britain. Compared with the Spitfire VB, the Mustang was faster up to 25,000 feet and had twice the range. However, the Spitfire VB could go much higher and had a better rate of climb and turn rate. It owed its superior high-altitude performance to its Rolls-Royce Merlin engine. When the RAF invited Rolls-Royce test pilot Ronnie Harker to fly the Mustang 1 at Duxford near Cambridge on 30 April 1942, he was impressed by its handling qualities, its fuel capacity (three times that of the Spitfire V) and by the positioning of the guns in the wings, which he felt gave greater accuracy of fire. His report to the RAF Air

Fighting Development Unit on the Mustang's general performance was very positive. In it, he suggested that a really special fighter might result if this exceptional airframe were to be combined with the proven, fuel-efficient Merlin engine. However, his report, and his subsequent lobbying of his Rolls-Royce officials and those of the Air Ministry, met with little enthusiasm. Few of them wanted anything to do with an American-built aircraft. Nonetheless, Harker persisted and was ultimately able to convince senior people at Rolls-Royce that his idea of mating the Merlin to the Mustang was not only likely to result in a wonderful new weapon against the Nazis, but would also produce a great deal of new engine business for the company. Executives at the engine manufacturer then persuaded the RAF to provide three Mustangs for Merlin installation at the Rolls-Royce Hucknall factory.

Next came a series of modifications, conversions and redesigns of the cowling and the cooling system, along with other detail changes. Finally, a Merlin 65-powered Mustang designated Mk X was produced, a highly successful realisation of Ronnie Harker's inspiration.

Rolls-Royce sent its performance and factory installation data on the Mk X to North American's design staff, who then began preliminary adaptive designs to incorporate the marvellous Merlin into production line Mustangs. Agreements were quickly reached with the Packard Motor Car Company and Continental Motors for the mass production of the V-12 Merlin engine in the United States under licence from Rolls-Royce, to supplement British production of the power plant. Among the many changes required by the Merlin-Mustang installation was the change to an enormous, four-bladed eleven foot two inch Hamilton Standard Hydromatic propeller.

In November 1942, General Henry 'Hap' Arnold was convinced by the promise of the rapidly developing Mustang and ordered more than 2,200 of the new fighters for the US Army Air Corps. By this time, North American was inundated with orders for its B-25 Mitchell medium bomber and AT-6 Texan/Harvard trainer, as well as for the Mustang, now designated P-51B. It began to construct expanded manufacturing facilities at Inglewood, a new plant for Mustang production in Dallas (the aircraft built there was designated P-51C, but was identical to the Inglewood product), and another new plant at Tulsa, Oklahoma.

Mustang production at the North American plants proceeded smoothly after initial delivery delays of Merlin engines from Packard were overcome. Performance testing of the early Merlin production aeroplanes proved the brilliance of Harker's idea. The new aircraft had a top speed of 441 mph, more than 50 mph faster than the Allison-powered Mustang. It showed greatly improved performance in virtually all other categories as well.

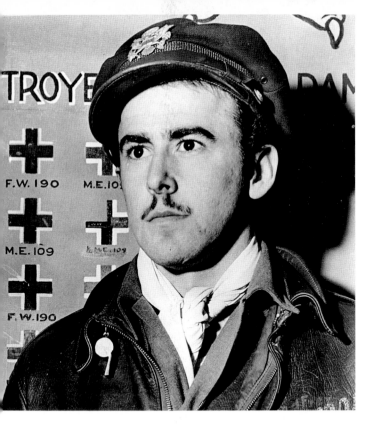

1. Captain John Godfrey at the 4th Fighter Group's Debden, England base in the Second World War. *(USAF)*

2. Captain Don Gentile in the cockpit of his P-51 Mustang. *Shangri-La*, at Debden, England, home to the 4th Fighter Group, Eighth USAAF, in the Second World War. *(USAF)*

3. Captain Don Gentile and his crew chief, S/Sgt. John Ferra, with their Mustang, *Shangri-La,* at the 336th Fighter Squadron dispersal, Debden, England. *(USAF)*

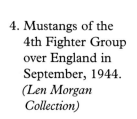

4. Mustangs of the 4th Fighter Group over England in September, 1944. *(Len Morgan Collection)*

5. Members of the
   336th Fighter
   Squadron, 4th
   Fighter Group, in
   their dispersal hut at
   Debden. *(USAF)*

6. Colonel Don
   Blakeslee, commander
   of the 4th Fighter
   Group, Eighth
   USAAF, Debden.
   (USAF)

7. 4th Fighter Group pilots listen intentley during a mission briefing at Debden in October 1943. *(Len Morgan*

8. Captain and Mrs Don Gentile. *(USAF)*

9. Captain John Godfrey, leaning against a wall of Vargas pin-ups at the 4FG's Debden base.
(USAF Museum)

10. Chorus girls of the famous Windmill Theatre, London, on the wing of a 4FG P-47 Thunderbolt fighter during a visit to the Debden base in June 1944.

(Len Morgan Collection)

11. An aerial view of the
    Debden base, circa 1944.
    (USAF Museum)

12. Captain Duane
    Beeson, left, 334th
    Fighter Squadron,
    4FG, and Captain
    Don Gentile. *(USAF)*

13. 'Captain Gentile watches as another enemy aircraft kill marking is added to his P-51. *(USAF)*

14. General Dwight D. Eisenhower awards the Distinguished Service Cross, the United States' second highest award for valour in combat, to 4FG commander Col. Don Blakeslee and Captain Don Gentile. *(USAF)*

15. Audley End Station, near Debden. Airmen of the 4th Fighter Group departed from here for London's Liverpool Street Station, on their occasional leaves.

(Len Morgan Collection)

16. Captain John Godfrey, left, and Captain Don Gentile at Gentile's Mustang. *(USAF)*

17. Captain Don Gentile at Debden, 1944. *(Piqua Public Library)*

18. 16-year-old Don Gentile and his first aeroplane, near his Piqua, Ohio home.
(courtesty Gregory Barbato)

19. Captain Gentile's homecoming,
    Piqua, Ohio, 20 May 1944.
    (courtesy Gregory Barbato)

20. Don Gentile, age 17, in Piqua.
    (courtesy Gregory Barbato)

21. Don Gentile in a friendly game at Debden, with Johnny Godfrey leaning on his shoulder. *(courtesy Gregory Barbato)*

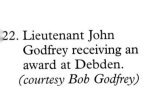

22. Lieutenant John Godfrey receiving an award at Debden. *(courtesy Bob Godfrey)*

23. Captains Godfrey, left,
and Gentile.
(courtesy Bob Godfrey)

24. John Godfrey, left, and
his brothers, circa 1926.
(courtesy Bob Godfrey)

25. John Godfrey and his
    P-47 Thunderbolt,
    Reggie's Reply, at
    Debden.
    (courtesy Bob Godfrey)

26. Post war, John Godfrey,
    left, and Don Gentile,
    representing Globe
    Aircraft.
    (courtesy Bob Godfrey)

27. On 7 March 1943, after a session of dog-fighting practice with another trainee pilot, Johnny Godfrey made a normal approach for a landing at his operational training unit base. Just as he was about to touch down, a strong crosswind caught his Spitfire. Struggling to regain control of the aircraft, he touched down and found that his brakes had failed. Roaring down the entire length of the runway, the Spitfire rolled off into mud at the end, the wheels dug in and the little fighter went over onto its nose. Godfrey was disgusted with himself. It was the first aircraft he had damaged since he had begun flying. *(courtesy Bob Godfrey)*

28. Johnny Godfrey and his P-47 Thunderbolt, *Reggie's Reply*. *(courtesy Bob Godfrey)*

29. In late February 1944, the 4th Fighter Group was transitioning from the P-47 Thunderbolt to the P-51 Mustang. This is the Mustang of 335th FS commander Major George Carpenter. *(courtesy Keith Hoey and Wade Meyers)*

30. General Jesse Auton pinning on award on the tunic of Captain Don Gentile at Debden. *(courtesy Bob Godfrey)*

The first American fighter group in the European Theatre of Operations to get the P-51B was the 354th Fighter Squadron, based at Boxted, Essex. Their Mustangs began arriving on 11 November 1943. Thereafter, the new fighters underwent field modification to prepare them for combat operations. These included the addition of external additional fuel capacity in the form of compressed paper and aluminium droppable tanks. Some Mustangs also received an 85 US gallon fuel tank in the fuselage right behind the pilot, as a field modification. This change became a production standard with the last 550 P-51Bs.

The Mustang encountered serious teething problems as it took on its primary role of long-range escort to the heavy bomber fleets of the US Eighth Air Force. Prolonged high-altitude operation soon resulted in the freezing of certain oils and greases, oxygen starvation, ice build-up on windscreens, coolant loss and resultant engine overheating, fouled spark plugs and jammed ammunition belts during high-G manoeuvres. All these problems were resolved, most of them in the field by energetic and creative crew chiefs. North American field representatives relayed information about the various problems and the fixes employed in the field to the company and modifications were soon incorporated into the production aeroplanes.

With the arrival of General James Doolittle as the new commander of the Eighth Air Force in January 1944, some of the escort Mustangs were released from their full-time commitment to the bombers they were shepherding. Instead, they were, for the first time, given the freedom to attack and destroy German fighters both before and after the Germans attacked the American bombers. Now, the Mustang began to show its true worth. More American fighter groups were being equipped with the slender, agile aircraft and by 3 March, when Mustangs first accompanied the bombers of the Eighth Air Force all the way to Berlin – a round trip of more than a thousand miles – the Americans knew that they finally had the long-range fighter they needed to defeat the *Luftwaffe*.

The diary of Lt Jack Raphael, 336th Fighter Squadron, details his first experiences with the Mustang:

19 February 1944 – Finally got to fly the Mustang. It's a sweet little plane. Really got a kick out of flying it. George flew it right after I did. The squadron started to do a balbo [mass formation flight], but it was recalled. Wehrman got back home from the hospital with his Purple Heart. New ultimatum issued requiring that all decorations be worn. Went to the late movie with George, had a bite to eat and headed for the house immediately after.

Captain Don Gentile recalled his combat flying in Mustangs with the
Fourth Fighter Group at Debden during 1944:

To show how a team works even when a big brawl has boiled the
team down to two men flying wing on each other, Johnny and I spent
twenty minutes over Berlin on March 8th and came out of there with
six planes destroyed to our credit. I got a straggler, and Johnny got
one, and then I got another one fast. A Hun tried to out-turn me, and
this was a mistake on his part. Not only can a Messerschmitt 109 not
out-turn a Mustang in the upstairs air, but even if he had succeeded,
there was Johnny back from his kill and sitting on my tail waiting to
shoot him down. He was waiting, too, to knock down anybody who
tried to bounce me off my kill.

There were Huns all around. Berlin's air was cloudy with them.
The gyrations this dying Hun was making forced me to violent
action, but Johnny rode right along like a blocking back who could
run with the best. After two Huns had blown up and another had
baled out, Johnny and I formed up tight and went against a team
of two Messerschmitts. 'I'll take the port one and you take the
starboard one,' I told Johnny, and we came in line abreast and in a
two-second burst finished off both of them. They were dead before
they knew we were there.

Then a Messerschmitt bounced Johnny. Johnny turned into him
and I swung around to run interference for him. The Hun made a
tight swing to get on Johnny's tail, saw me and rolled right under me
before I could get a shot in. I rolled with him and fastened to his tail,
but by that time we were very close to flak coming up from the city.
The Hun wasn't so worried about the flak. I was his immediate and
more desperate woe, but flak wasn't my idea of cake to eat, and I
didn't dare go slow in it while the Hun took a chance and put his flaps
down to slow to a crawl.

Then I got strikes on him. Glycol started coming out of him, and I
had to pass him. But Johnny had fallen into formation right on my
wing and he took up the shooting where I had left off. He put more
bullets into the Hun while I was swinging up and around to run
interference for him. Then he said his ammunition had run out and I
said, 'Okay, I'll finish him,' and I followed the Nazi down into the
streets clobbering him until he pulled up and baled out.

The whole thing goes in a series of whooshes. There is no time to
think. If you take time to think, you will not have time to act. There
are a number of things your mind is doing while you are fighting –
seeing, measuring, guessing, remembering, adding up this and that

and worrying about one thing and another and taking this into account and that into account and rejecting this notion and accepting that notion. But it doesn't feel like thinking.

After the fight is over you can look back on all the things you did and didn't do and see the reason behind each move. But while the fight is on, your mind feels empty and feels as if the flesh of it is sitting in your head, bunched up like muscle and quivering there.

I remember . . . after I had run my score of destroyed to thirty, with twenty-three in the air and seven on the ground, we were over Schweinfurt. There were three Messerschmitts just sitting up there in front of me and not noticing me – just presenting themselves as the easiest shots I have had in this war so far. I was positive I was going to get all three.

Then I saw a Hun clobbering a Mustang mate of mine. I dropped my easy kills and dove on the Hun to bounce him off that Mustang. I didn't think about it at all; it was just a reflex action – nor do I regret having such reflexes. If the feeling for team action had not been developed as a reflex in me – something I and all the other boys can do without thinking – then I would have been dead or a prisoner of war a long time ago.

Captain Johnny Godfrey recalled his first experiences with the Mustang:

Rumours had been flying hot and heavy that we were being transferred from P-47s to P-51s. We had heard a lot of talk about this amazing plane. By cutting the fire power to four machine-guns and using a new type of carburettor, it was capable of 1,800 mile flights with its two belly tanks. Our P-47s had only one belly tank, which was slung underneath the fuselage. The 51s had them slung under each wing, with two more permanent tanks in the wing and another tank just to the rear of the cockpit.

On February 22nd, the rumours became a fact; one P-51 landed and we were all (sixty pilots) ordered to fly it in preparation for the changeover. It was a beautiful airplane; it reminded me of the Spitfire with its huge in-line engine. And, like the Spitfire, it too was glycol-cooled. We queued up on the plane like housewives at a bargain sale. The time in the air was spread very thin, forty minutes was all the time I had in the air in a 51 when on the morning of the 28th the group flew to Steeple Morden in their P-47s and traded them for P-51s. The planes didn't have their auxiliary tanks on, but they were full of fuel and the machine-guns were loaded. Our briefing was held on the ground among our 51s. No flying back to Debden for us, but off on a fighter sweep to France. We were familiarising ourselves with this plane the hard way.

The Air Force had made no mistake when they made their purchase of Mustangs from the North American Aviation Company. They were the hottest planes in the skies. From zero to 30,000 feet they were able to match anything the German Air Force put into the air. If the fighting spirit of the group was high before the advent of the 51, it was now at fever pitch. But horrible little bugs were plaguing the 51s – motor trouble, gas trouble, radio trouble – and the worst bug of all, besides our windows frosting up, was in our machine-guns. At high altitudes they froze up on us; moreover, in a dogfight they were often jammed by the force of gravity in a turn. That meant straightening out before firing, a feat that was practically impossible under the circumstances. Technicians were rushed to the base to iron out our problems. The war was still going on and the great air offensive against Germany was now in full swing, so we had to fly them, bugs and all.

Major Walter Konantz, 55th Fighter Group, recalled:

On September 11th 1944 we were escorting B-17s to Ruhland and were approaching the rendezvous point at 25,000 feet when I had to use the relief tube. In order to use the tube (which is vented overboard), it was necessary to unbuckle the lap belt and shoulder harness as well as the leg straps of the parachute and slide well forward on the seat. I was in this position when a voice came over the radio shouting, 'Me 109s, here they come'. I looked up and saw about fifty Me 109s diving through our formation and firing. One crossed in front of me in a 45 dive and was firing at a P-51 below and to my left. This was the first time I had ever seen an enemy aircraft and, with a case of 'buck fever', I peeled off and went after him. He saw me chasing him and steepened his dive to vertical. I was also headed straight down with full power. Both of us descended from 25,000 feet at extremely high speed. Being completely unstrapped, I was a free-floating object in the cockpit and my body was at zero Gs. The slightest movement of the stick would cause me to leave the seat and hit the canopy. The airplane was very touchy at this speed and at times I felt like a basketball being dribbled down the court.

We both started to pull out at about 8,000 feet. I glanced at my airspeed indicator which, at that moment, was showing 600 miles per hour, 95 miles per hour over the red line speed. The Me 109 had only completed about 45 degrees of his pull up when his right wing came off through the wheel well area. He spun into the ground in a few seconds with no time to bale out. Even though no one else saw this victory, nor did I have any of it on the gun camera film, I still got credit for it due to the fact that one of the other pilots had counted the fires on the ground after the huge fifteen minute dogfight and reported to the debriefing officer that he counted thirty fires. There were claims of twenty-eight Me 109s shot down with the loss of two P-51s. After landing, when I had stepped out onto the wing, my crew chief remarked, 'Better zip up your pants before you go in for debriefing.'

Merle Olmsted was a Mustang crew chief with the 357th Fighter Group at Leiston, England. He recalled his experiences with the Mustang:

When ground crews are mentioned, which is seldom, the reference is usually to the crew chiefs. Most Eighth Air Force fighter units assigned three men to each airplane. Besides the crew chief, there was an assistant crew chief and an armament man. Their first duty on arriving at the plane was to remove the cockpit and wing covers and Pitot tube cover. Then the propeller was pulled through its arc a few times and the pre-flight inspection was started. The P-51 is remarkably simple. Nevertheless, the pre-flight, as laid out in the manual, is quite lengthy. Most of it consists of visual inspections, many of which were completed during the post-flight inspection the day before. All reservoirs were checked for fluid level, coolant, hydraulics, battery, engine oil and fuel. An inspection was always made under the aircraft for coolant leaks, which frequently occurred due to temperature changes. It was often difficult to tell coolant from water, but tasting a bit of the fluid with the tongue will reveal the difference, as coolant has a bitter taste (and is poisonous if consumed in quantity).

If all visual and servicing checks were satisfactory, the engine run was done, using the battery cart to save the airplane's internal battery. Because the seat is rather deep to accommodate the pilot's dinghy pack, a cushion in the seat helped one to reach the brakes and to see out from the cockpit. Now the brakes were set and the seatbelt fastened around the control stick to provide 'up elevators' during the power check. The flaps were left down, the fuel selector was set to either main tank, the throttle cracked open, and the mixture control set to the idle cut-off position. After yelling 'clear' to be sure no one was near the nose of the plane, the starter switch was engaged (the P-51 has a direct-drive starter), along with engine prime. As soon as the cylinders began to fire, the mixture control was moved to 'run'. The propeller was already in 'full increase rpm' for the warm-up. Various additional checks were carried out, including checking that the engine oil and coolant temperature instruments were registering in 'the green'. The engine was run up to 2,300 rpm and the magnetos checked. With each mag off, the maximum allowable rpm drop is 100. The propeller governor was also checked at this rpm. The maximum rpm is 3,000, but this is for take-off and was not used on the ground run.

After the engine was shut down and everything had checked out OK, it was mostly a matter of waiting. The fuel and oil trucks cruised the perimeter track and all tanks were topped up after the run. Now the windshield, canopy and rear-view mirror were all polished – for the tenth time. The armament man had long since charged his guns, so all aircraft on the field had 'hot' guns long before take-off. The gun switches in the cockpit were off, of course, but occasionally one was left on and the pilot gripping the stick could fire a burst, terrifying everyone within range, including himself.

The pilots usually arrived fifteen to twenty minutes before engine start time, via an overloaded jeep or weapons carrier. After the pilot was strapped in with the help of the ground crew, his goggles and the windshield were given a final swipe. Engine start time comes and sixty Merlins coughed into life around the airfield hardstands. Then the wheel chocks were pulled and, with a wave of his hand to the ground crew, each pilot guided his Mustang out to the proper place on the taxi track in a snake-like procession toward the active runway.

The ground crews, and everyone else in the airfield area, sought a vantage point to watch the take-off, always an exciting event. The sight and sound of sixty or more overloaded Mustangs getting airborne was impressive.

Much of the weight the planes were carrying was represented by two long-range fuel drop tanks, so vital to the success of the US fighters in Europe. Most of these tanks were made of paper composition units, each holding 108 US gallons and built in huge quantities by British companies. They were installed on the wing racks for the next day's mission the night before and were filled at that time. During operation they were pressurised to ensure positive feeding at altitude, by the exhaust side of the engine vacuum pump. The piping for this and the fuel flow is rubber tubes with glass elbows, which broke away cleanly when the tanks were dropped. Even though the drop tanks are pressurised, it was necessary to coax fuel into the system during the pre-flight. After switching to the 'drop tank' position, the engine would often die and the selector switch had to quickly be put back to 'main' and then to 'drop tanks' until they fed properly. On the mission they were always dropped when empty, or earlier if combat demanded it. With all fifteen fighter groups operating, Eighth Air Force fighters could require 1,800 drop tanks per day.

At mid-day, while the mission aircraft were out, the line crews were in a state of suspended animation. It was mostly free time, time to attend to laundry, read the squadron bulletin board to see when mail call was, and to see if your name has appeared on any unwanted, but unavoidable, extra duty rosters. There was also time to drop into the post exchange for a candy bar, and to take in noon chow at the big consolidated mess hall.

Regardless of what they had been doing while the mission was out, the aircraft ground crew would always 'sweat out' the return of their particular airplane and pilot, and when both returned safely it was a great relief.

Whether a crew had a close relationship with their pilot depended on several factors – how long they had been together, the pilot's general attitude towards enlisted men, and if he was an outgoing individual.

Although the word 'hero' probably never occurred to the ground crews, they were well aware that it was their pilot who was doing the fighting, and sometimes the dying. In most cases, there was considerable affection for their pilot and they were proud of his achievements. There was always a period of depression when an aircraft and pilot failed to return from a mission, and often the cause didn't filter down to the ground crew. In a day or two, a new P-51 arrived, and a new pilot, and the war went on.

An average mission of the 357th Fighter Group lasted about four to five hours and by the ETR (estimated time of return) everyone was back on the hardstands. If the group came into sight in proper formation and to the rising snarl of many Merlins, it was probable that there had been no combat. If they straggled back in small groups, or individually, it was certain that there had been some kind of action. Missing red tape around the gun muzzles was a final confirmation.

As each P-51 turned into its parking place, the pilot blasted the tail around and shut down the engine, the wheels were chocked and the mission was over – one more toward the completion of his tour.

Now he brought any aircraft malfunctions to the attention of his
ground crew, and left for debriefing. For the ground crews there was
considerable work ahead to complete the post-flight inspection and
repair the aircraft. If luck was with them, their airplane could be 'put
to bed' in time for evening chow, and the work day would have come
to an end. Often, though, it did not work out that way, and their jobs
continued into the night.

The fourteen months on Eighth Fighter Command's Leiston
airfield was a unique experience for the ground crews, and probably
the high point of life for many. Most of us, however, did not
appreciate this at the time, and wanted only to get it over with and go
home. Only in later years did some realise what a fascinating time
it had been, and many of us have returned several times to the now
tranquil land that once housed a fighter group at war.

In an effort to improve their already splendid air weapon, North American
modified a P-51B from its Inglewood line to carry a bubble or 'teardrop'
canopy. This modification greatly enhanced the pilot's visibility. The
canopy became the most notable feature of the next Mustang version, the
P-51D, which also featured a strengthened airframe, a standard 85-US
gallon fuselage fuel tank, a slightly modified cowling, a modified landing
gear, wing armament standardised to six .50-calibre Browning machine-
guns, and a V-1650-7 Merlin engine of 1695 hp (war emergency rating).
The D models soon began arriving at the American squadrons in England
and other war theatres.

The widespread availability of this newest and most highly evolved
Mustang gave the fighter groups a new target priority. If German aircraft
could be successfully attacked and destroyed while still parked on their
airfields, and if their hangars, runways and other airfield facilities
could be rendered unserviceable, the Allied cause in the air war would be
considerably advanced. Jimmy Doolittle was quick to support this new
priority by releasing some P-51 squadrons to hit the enemy airfields and
other surface targets. The Mustangs proved extremely effective in this
added role, but at a heavy price. For the remainder of the war in Europe,
significantly more P-51s were lost to German ground fire than to aerial
combat. The *Luftwaffe* was efficient at defending its airfields, which
were ringed with anti-aircraft weapons. The Mustangs were particularly
vulnerable to hits in the cooling system; many were shot to pieces or
brought down by shrapnel hits to the radiator or cooling tubes while
attacking German aerodromes. In spite of the increased losses to ground
fire, the Mustang was considered quite effective in the ground-attack role,
if somewhat less so than the heavier, radial-engined, P-47 Thunderbolt.

As dominant as the P-51 had quickly become in the skies over German-occupied Europe, its pilots were soon facing fearsome new weaponry from the other side. Jet and rocket-propelled fighters in the form of the Messerschmitt Me 262 and Me 163 respectively, were appearing with increasing frequency in the defence of the Reich, and their performance, though limited and erratic, was startling and devastating. They sliced through the American bomber formations, often destroying two or more heavy bombers in a single pass. But while the speed and performance of the Me 262, for example, was considerably superior to that of the Mustang, they were never available in sufficient numbers to the *Luftwaffe* to overcome the powerful presence of the P-51s. In the Pacific, the new Boeing B-29 Superfortress long-range bombers, with their massive incendiary loads, were starting to bring the terror and fury of the man-made firestorm to the Japanese home islands, which were fiercely defended by their fighter force. This was the supreme test for the P-51D. It was required to escort the B-29s over thousands of miles of lonely, cruel sea. An oft-quoted remark about the early Superfortresses was 'three turning, one burning', in reference to their inclination toward engine fire problems. The Mustangs frequently had to escort B-29s crippled by mechanical failure, while simultaneously fending off the attacks of Japanese fighters looking for easy pickings among the bombers. Still, the B-29s efficiently practised their fire-bombing technique on more than sixty key Japanese target cities, all but burning them to a fine ash by the end of the war. They were accompanied to and from their objectives by P-51s operating mainly from a precious little SeaBee-built airfield on the hard-won island of Iwo Jima. It was from Iwo Jima that the Mustangs took final control of the airspace over Japan, which they maintained until the atomic bombing of Hiroshima and Nagasaki ended the Pacific War in August 1945.

The Mustang continued to be developed through a succession of variants until the end of the Second World War and was undoubtedly, at that point, the most successful and highly regarded fighter in the history of aviation. By the end of the war, Mustangs of the USAAF, the RAF and the other Allied air forces, had destroyed nearly 5,000 enemy aircraft in the European theatre alone. The combat life of the aircraft continued in the Korean War of 1950, in the Arab-Israeli wars and in other conflicts of many different air forces.

More than 200 Mustangs are still flown today world-wide – careful, loving restorations by proud enthusiasts who continue to appreciate the charms and performance of an aeroplane that many believe contributed more to victory in the Second World War than any other.

Ed Schmued, the quiet, modest, brilliant designer of the Mustang, died of heart failure on Saturday 1 June 1985, aged eighty-five. He was cremated and, on 15 June, at the request of his widow Christel, his ashes were flown from Los Angeles International Airport out to sea, where they were scattered. Ed's last flight took place in a Mustang, the aeroplane he created and loved to the end of his days.

In January 1944 the rumour mill at Debden was working overtime. Word had it that, at long last, the group would soon be trading in their P-47 Thunderbolts for the P-51 Mustang. The pilots had been hearing a lot about the Mustang. They had heard that by using a new type of carburettor, reducing the number of machine-guns from six to four, and with two underwing drop tanks in addition to two permanent fuel tanks in the wings and another tank to the rear of the cockpit, the sleek new fighter was capable of flying an 1,800 mile mission.

On 22 February 1944 a P-51 landed at Debden and all of the group's sixty pilots were ordered to fly it. Their conversion to Mustangs was imminent. With its graceful, streamlined design and Packard-Merlin in-line engine, the aircraft reminded the pilots of the Spitfires they had flown before having to change over to Thunderbolts. With so many pilots queued up to fly the new fighter, most of them got a mere thirty to forty minutes in the air with it before the morning of 28 February. On this date the entire group flew their P-47s over to nearby Steeple Morden in Cambridgeshire and traded them for brand-new P-51s. The Mustangs lacked their auxiliary drop tanks, but were fully fuelled and loaded with ammunition for their .50-calibre guns.

The new aircraft would clearly be all they had hoped for in a new fighter – the hottest plane in the sky from zero altitude to 30,000 feet. It was every bit as good or better than the best the Germans could put up against it. But in the early days and weeks of transition, a lot of problems arose. The group called for help and technicians came quickly to Debden and, in consultation with the crew chiefs, soon resolved them.

On 3 March 1944 the Fourth Fighter Group flew the first escorted bombing raid on Berlin. It was the longest mission to date for the fighters and bombers of the Eighth Air Force. Until the arrival of the Mustang, such a mission would have been impossible to mount. The aeroplane was still suffering teething problems, however, and the weather was deteriorating badly. So badly, in fact, that Eighth Bomber Command elected to abort the mission and notified the bombers to return to their bases. Blakeslee, codenamed Horseback, radioed to the pilots of the Fourth Fighter Group that the mission had been cancelled and to return to base. However, the message was received by only about half of the

Debden pilots. The others, Major Halsey, Captain Gentile and Lieutenants Millikan, Carlson, Herter, Godfrey, Garrison, Barnes and Dunn continued blithely on and into a light cloud formation as the weather went from bad to worse. When they emerged from the cloud, they ran smack into a force of sixty German aircraft . . . Bf 109s, Me 210s and Fw 190s. The Mustangs were instantly immersed in the enemy swarm and had to fight in the midst of the impossible odds. There was no possibility of operating in the standard leader and wingman units. It was every man for himself. For Johnny Godfrey it was the greatest scare of his young career as a fighter pilot. One of the newer Fw 190s, the long-nose variety, would certainly have shot him down if Johnny had been anything less than utterly ham-fisted in throwing his P-51 around the sky in the encounter. He survived – and learned a few new tricks about dogfighting.

From the diary of Lt Jack Raphael, 336th Fighter Squadron:

3 March 1944 – Got called before dawn again. Briefed for a show to BERLIN! Didn't go as I was on the last trip. Pappy Dunn flew my 51. Nine of our boys were jumped by about 150 Fw 190s and Me 109s over Berlin. Herter, Dunn and Barnes missing. Gentile destroyed two, Carlson one, and Millikan one. Garrison shot down by flak over Boulogne. Show was 1,296 miles long! First time Allied fighters over Berlin. Spent part of the afternoon in the ARC Club and the darkroom. Stayed in the mess for a short time after supper and then came back to the room to write a couple of letters. Goody got his gold leaves and Doug Hobert started wearing his railroad tracks.

The next day the Eighth Air Force tried again to hit Berlin. Of the sixteen Fourth Fighter Group Mustangs to take off from Debden that morning, only three were able to rendezvous with the bomber force and continue with them to the target and back to England. All the other fighters of Blakeslee's force suffered engine, radio and other problems, requiring them to abort the mission.

Bob Richards was flying on Godfrey's wing as they headed east across the Channel. He called Johnny on the RT: 'Hello, Shirt Blue Red Leader, this is Red Two. My motor's acting up. Am returning to base.' 'Roger, Red Two,' Johnny replied. Bob turned back. Very soon, as his Mustang approached the Dutch coast, Johnny was startled when his own engine began to cough and splutter. Now it was his turn to abort. The weather over much of England was terrible as he crossed the coast heading for Debden. He had been letting down through cloud while over the Channel but experienced icing and decided to turn east again while continuing to descend. He finally broke through the cloud base at about 700 feet and went on in to Debden. On landing he learned that Bob had not yet returned. Johnny was not particularly concerned at that point, thinking that his friend had probably landed at Martlesham Heath or some other airfield nearer to the coast. An hour or so later, as he sat in the 336th Fighter Squadron dispersal hut, the phone rang. It was answered by Mac, the intelligence officer. Mac then offered Johnny an extra shot of mission whiskey, saying: 'Here, Johnny, this is a bonus day. Have another drink. Somebody's got to tell you and I guess I'm the one. A call just came through from the RAF. Bob's plane crashed at Framlingham. He was still in the cockpit. He's dead, Johnny.'

The constable's report from East Suffolk Police read:

I beg to report that at 1130 hours Saturday, 4th March 1944, an American P-51 Mustang Fighter plane, marked VFI (36786) Home Station-Debden, crashed in a field about 800 yards SW of Durban's Farm, Framlingham. The 'plane was completely smashed but did not catch fire, wreckage was scattered over a wide area. It was piloted by Lt R. H. Richards, age 23, who was killed, his body was found near the wreckage. The USAAF Station, Parham, was informed and the body removed to that station. The fields concerned are in the occupation of Mr Cecil Randall, Red House Farm, Kettleburgh. There was no damage to civilian property. PHQ & DHQ informed by telephone.

Johnny Godfrey recalled the funeral:

Our base chaplain made all the arrangements for Bob's funeral. The bus that was to take us to the cemetery was waiting in front of the officers' mess at 10:30. Mrs C., JJ, Jimmy Goodson – Bob's CO, Bob's crew chief, the boys from the orchestra, Lieutenant Charlotte Fredericks and three other nurses from the nearby hospital all climbed in for the ride [to Madingley] cemetery twenty miles away, near the city of Cambridge. It was a quiet and sad journey. JJ and I sat together, but we were each preoccupied with our own thoughts and very few words were spoken.

The chapel was surrounded by a carefully cut lawn on which were hundreds of white crosses in neat little rows. There were no other stone markers or tombs, only the bleak little crosses on which name, rank and serial number were painted in black letters, showing the final resting place of American airmen. When we entered the chapel a pine box completely covered by the American flag was resting near the altar. This held the remains of Bob's mangled body. As a house of God it lacked the spiritual feeling of churches I had been accustomed to. It was not a church of life, where marriages and baptisms were blessed – and the atmosphere seemed haunted by the young souls whose lives were taken away from them in the bloom of youth. The prayers were not too long, for we had been a little late in arriving, and the schedule of burial services was timed in a cold and impersonal manner. No sooner was Bob's coffin carried out, than another one took its place in this church of the dead.

'Ashes to ashes and dust to dust,' the chaplain said, and with the faint sounds of the bugle beginning The Last Call, Bob's body was lowered into the ground. We stood there, all of us clinging to the memory of Bob as we last remembered him. From far off in the distance the second bugle answered in a mournful call to a soldier on his last journey.

From the diary of Lt Jack Raphael, 336th Fighter Squadron:

7 March 1944 – At last a release came through for maintenance and training. Weather dull all morning. Saw some combat films. Had a 'B' flight bull session. During the afternoon went to Bob Richards' funeral as a pall bearer. We were all sorry to see such a damn fine fellow go. Went to the late movie with Gentile, Goody, Bonds and Megura.

CHAPTER EIGHT

Horseback

From the diary of 1st Lt Jack Raphael, 336th Fighter Squadron:

1 February 1944 – Released all day because of duff weather. Got some enlarging paper from Mom and a couple of good pipes from Louie. Good show! Went to presentation during afternoon. Grover, Goodson, Gentile and Blakeslee got OLC to DFC. and Blakeslee got his Silver Star. Godfrey got hell for wearing a raunchy cap! George and I played cards after supper and puttered around our rooms. Wrote some letters.

Most historians, and most fighter pilots that flew in the European Theatre of Operations in the Second World War, would probably agree that the two truly great American fighter group leaders of that campaign were Colonel Hubert 'Hub' Zemke and Colonel Donald Blakeslee. Hub Zemke was born in Missoula, Montana, on 14 March 1914, the only child of German immigrants Anna and Benno Zemke. Hub grew up in a rough part of town and during and after the First World War, the Zemkes were subjected to a high degree of anti-German hostility. This was exacerbated by the young boy's limited English, owing to the family speaking only German at home. As a teenager, Hub became interested in boxing and, initially for reasons of self-defence; he quickly learned and excelled at the sport. He eventually became Montana State middleweight champion for two years.

Following early military exposure in the university Reserve Officer Training Corps, Hub applied and was accepted for aviation cadet training in the US Army Air Corps, ultimately emerging as a fighter pilot, an officer and a gentleman. By the end of 1940, with war raging in Europe, he was sent to England as a USAAC observer of the air war. There, he was able to fly and evaluate a number of British front-line aircraft, including the Spitfire, Hurricane and Blenheim.

In September 1942, after a brief period in Russia, instructing Soviet pilots on flying the Curtiss P-40 Tomahawk fighter, Hub was finally given command of his own fighter group, the 56th, which was newly operational in England. The group would become famous as 'the Wolf Pack' and Hub gained wide respect and fame for his tactics and effectiveness as an air leader of high standards and great integrity. Through much of the European air war, Zemke's Wolf Pack and Don Blakeslee's Fourth Fighter Group traded the lead in the race for the top-scoring American fighter organisation. Whether the 4th or the 56th would finally have prevailed in that race will never be known. Hub became a prisoner-of-war as a result of an escort mission on 30 October 1944. However, his achievement as a superb fighter leader, and later as a fine Allied camp leader in Stalag Luft 1, is beyond dispute.

Don Blakeslee was a native of Fairport Harbor, Ohio. Like Zemke, Blakeslee was a genius at putting his pilots in position to destroy enemy aircraft. Who was the better fighter pilot? Blakeslee was the better flier, but Zemke was the better shot. Their greatness lay in their 'generalship'. Of the two, Grover Hall wrote:

> Top-flight pilots of the 4th could shoot better than Blakeslee. 'Hell, I can't hit the side of a barn. There's no sport in it for a guy who can shoot straight. The sport comes when somebody like me has to pull up behind 'em and start shooting to find out where the bullets are going – like spraying flowers with a garden hose.' Each shot down a formidable string of Jerries, but their forte was leadership. Each was the generator of his group. Zemke was a well-rounded officer, energetic, relatively polished, reticent but not forbidding. Contrarily, Blakeslee was ill at ease in the administrative sphere of his command. He was rapacious, explosive, easy to drink and jest with, but difficult to understand.

It is believed that Blakeslee, who unquestionably led from the front, accumulated more combat flying hours than any other American fighter pilot. His radio call sign, as group leader in the air, was Horseback. With somewhere between 400 and 500 missions, he finished the war with more than 1,000 hours of operational flying. He told his men that they should turn head-on into an attack by enemy fighters and under no circumstance should they deviate from this course of action. One young lieutenant enquired: 'But Colonel, what if the German doesn't break either?' With an icy stare, Blakeslee replied: 'Then, sonny, you will have just earned your hazardous duty pay.' At one point in his command of the Fourth Fighter Group, he was quoted as saying: 'We love fighting. Fighting is a grand sport.'

On 16 August 1943 the Fourth Fighter Group was escorting the B-17s of the 1st Bomb Division to a target in the Paris area. When the group arrived at the rendezvous point, it found that the bombers were already under attack by enemy fighters. Blakeslee led his charges into the action and, in an air battle lasting nearly an hour, they destroyed eighteen German aircraft – the highest loss the enemy had suffered in a single day of the air war. The success of the Fourth Fighter Group pilots that day is largely attributable to the excellent direction they received from Blakeslee orbiting above the battle. It was one of the first occasions where he demonstrated his gift for leading and directing his men to outstanding success against the fighter pilots of the *Luftwaffe*.

Great Sampford was one of the satellite airfields for the main station of Debden. No. 133 Eagle Squadron was based there prior to its move to Debden. When he was appointed commander of No. 133 Eagle Squadron (well before the three Eagle Squadrons were transferred into the USAAF to become the Fourth Fighter Group), Don Blakeslee introduced himself to his pilots in the bar at 1 am (according to ace Jim Goodson) by announcing that the drinks were on him. He then added that all pilots were to report for a briefing at 6 am Goodson recalled:

> [Blakeslee] . . . was a great believer in the RAF tradition of hard drinking and high living, and never permitting either of them to interfere with constant readiness to fly, and fly well, at any time.

While still at Great Sampford, it is fair to say that morale among the pilots of No. 133 Eagle Squadron was low. Some of the pilots were also smarting at being stuck in poor facilities while the men of the other two Eagle squadrons were enjoying the comparative luxury of the Debden main base. Making the situation worse was the Great Sampford airfield itself, which was small, grass, oddly shaped and had an uneven surface. The pilots were accustomed to taking off in pairs – a leader and his wingman. Goodson recalled:

> On a very good field, I had seen a section of four scrambled off at the same time. Only twice had I ever seen a whole squadron of sixteen aircraft take off in formation: once on the huge grass airfield at Martlesham Heath, and once at the big main airfield at Tangmere.

Perhaps the point of the exercise was to instil a bit of squadron pride in the pilots of No. 133 Fighter Squadron; or maybe it was just Blakeslee being Blakeslee. On the last day of their residency at Great Sampford, the CO ordered that all the aircraft should taxi out and form up on the east perimeter of the field. 'When I give the signal, the squadron will take off in formation!' Before anyone in the room could react, Blakeslee rumbled, 'Move!'

They taxied into position in the pre-dawn darkness, every pilot struggling to keep from chewing up a nearby aircraft with his propeller. They had to keep zigging and zagging to see around the long, obscuring noses of their Spitfires as they worried about the big Merlin engines overheating in prolonged ground manoeuvring. Then Blakeslee raised and brought his arm forward and they were off. For all of the pilots behind the leading aircraft, there was the nerve-wracking jockeying of throttles as they worked to hold position and yet maintain sufficient ground speed to clear the fence that was looming at the boundary of the short field. Several of the fighters were forced to swerve on take-off to avoid the trees beyond the fence.

Blakeslee said, 'Tighten it up. Let's show these bastards!' As he spoke, the entire squadron was approaching the airfield at Debden, at less than 500 feet, so close was their satellite field to the main base. It must have been a powerful vision for those on the ground who witnessed that mass of elegant Spitfires suddenly appear over the near horizon and flash across the field and out of sight almost before they realised what had just happened. Goodson recalled:

The formation was even better when we came back over the base at Debden, peeled off and landed at Great Sampford. It was when we climbed out of the planes that I understood. There was excitement, enthusiasm, boasting, and pride. Everyone was babbling about how, against all odds, they faced and overcame catastrophe and gave a show fit for heroes. That evening Blakeslee wasn't the only 133 pilot with the belligerent swagger as we arrived in the officers' mess at Debden. It had become a squadron characteristic, and the other squadrons accepted it. Next day we left Great Sampford and moved into the main base at Debden.

When the Eagles were transferred to the USAAF and reformed as the Fourth Fighter Group, they were initially commanded by Wing Commander Raymond Duke-Woolley, on loan from the RAF. Duke-Woolley was soon succeeded by the highly experienced former Eagle leader, Chesley 'Pete' Peterson. He led the pilots of the Fourth Fighter Group until 1 January 1944, when Don Blakeslee took over.

Blakeslee had come to England in May 1941 and was sent to RAF Digby in Lincolnshire. Here, he earned the wrath of the RAF CO by refusing to march the enlisted men to Sunday morning worship, insisting that that chore should be for non-flying officers. The American was 'punished' by being posted to RAF Biggin Hill, south of London. There, he finished his 200-hour operational tour of duty and was about to be made an instructor. He discovered that he could stay on combat flying status by transferring to one of the Eagle Squadrons, whose members he openly disrespected. Still, he chose their company in preference to being taken off combat ops, even serving briefly as commander of No. 133 (Eagle) Squadron, where he built up his combat flying hours to 400.

Apart from the leadership, the most significant difference between the Fourth and 56th Fighter Groups was in their attitudes about the aircraft they flew. The 56th had trained hard with, and developed an affinity for, the Republic P-47 Thunderbolt. They took it into combat and became extremely successful with it. The Fourth Fighter Group, on the other hand, had grown up with the lovely in-line engined Spitfire and found little to love about the big Thunderbolt. They missed the lithe, subtle handling of the little British fighter and yearned for the Mustang, of which they had heard so much. Blakeslee, perhaps more than anyone in the Fourth Fighter Group, wanted the North American machine for his group – the aeroplane that was to become the most successful fighter of the war.

The first of the new Packard-Merlin-engined Mustangs arrived in England in November 1943, going straight to the 354th Fighter Group of the American Ninth Air Force. General William Kepner chose the experienced Don Blakeslee to lead the 354th Fighter Group into combat with their new P-51s. Blakeslee was already a combat veteran and well qualified to compare the Mustang with the Thunderbolt, then in wide use in the ETO. While temporarily assigned to the 354th Fighter Group at Boxted, Blakeslee flew his borrowed Mustang back to Debden each night and witnessed the enthusiasm and envy the aeroplane aroused in the pilots of the Fourth Fighter Group. They couldn't wait to get their hands on the new aircraft.

After that assignment, Blakeslee went to work on Kepner, lobbying hard for the replacement of the Fourth Fighter Group's Thunderbolts with the Mustangs. In general, Kepner agreed with the wisdom of Blakeslee's request, but was concerned about taking the Fourth Fighter Group out of combat ops for a period of transition training of the pilots and ground crews on the new aircraft. The American bomber offensive was at a critical point and he was loath to withdraw any fighter escort capability from the bombers. Blakeslee is said to have asked the general how much time he could have to make the switch from P-47s to P-51s. The answer was twenty-four hours and Blakeslee agreed to it. The group got its Mustangs and, true to his word, Blakeslee and the pilots of the Fourth Fighter Group took them directly to the Continent on a mission.

With the P-51, Don Blakeslee and the Fourth Fighter Group pilots broke all the records and, perhaps more than any other flying organisation of the USAAF, established American air superiority and then supremacy in the skies over Europe. Probably the zenith of Blakeslee's career leading the group came with the pioneering England–Russia–Italy shuttle escort mission of 21 June 1944 – the longest day of the year in more ways than one. It was to be a 1,600-mile flight, from Debden to a remote field in the Russian Steppes – the longest of long-ranging missions for the group and its marvellous Mustangs. According to Grover Hall, unlike many American fighter pilots Blakeslee never painted swastika markers on his aircraft to show the number of enemy planes he had downed and he never painted a name on his aircraft to personalise it. He also had no interest in other fighter pilot affectations, such as wearing a white silk scarf or a decorated A2 leather flying jacket. However, on that first shuttle mission, he did elect to wear the scarf.

The shuttle was being flown just two weeks after the D-Day landings at Normandy and was designed to damage German morale further and to boost that of the Russians. The Fourth Fighter Group was to escort 104 B-17s on a mission to attack an oil refinery south of Berlin. Meanwhile, another force of 1,001 bombers went to Berlin on one of the largest 'diversionary efforts' in history, to draw enemy defensive interest away from the smaller force. In the briefing at Debden, Blakeslee told his pilots:

Now look, before we all get excited about it, I'll say the whole trip is about seven and a half hours. We've done 'em that long before. We'll be throttled back, so Christ, we could stay up for eight hours. There'll be 1,001 bombers acting as diversion for our 104 bombers! We'll take the bombers up to the Russian frontier, from there it's 258 miles to base. We should be met by Russian fighter planes – Yaks. I'll be leading with 336th Squadron. On the way to Russia – we will not – we will not – do any fighting on the way over. You will not drop your tanks. If you are attacked, go into a turn with 'em. If for any reason you should have to drop tanks around Berlin – you've had it. You'll have to return to Debden.

I want to land sixty-eight aircraft at this place [pointing at map]. You're safe here if you're not straggling. The Russians are sensitive to stragglers. Several reconnaissance craft were shot up recently. You don't have to worry about Russian fighters over 15,000 feet – that's their ceiling.

Once we rendezvous with the bombers, there will be absolutely no radio conversation. If you see a man's wing on fire – just be quiet, he'll find out about it himself after a while.

Let's make a pretty landing, a pansy landing, bang, bang, bang. We want to make the thing look like a seven and a half-hour trip is nothing to us. There are no replacements, so if you crack up your plane, that means you probably stay in Russia for the rest of the war.

For Christ's sake, no landing errors. The Russians shoot the men who make mistakes – when in Russia do as the Russians do.

No one will take a gun. If you're forced down – a gun is a death warrant. No guns at all. I don't know whether I'd even let them catch me with a knife. Too much like a weapon. Now these guerrillas are trying to recruit men to fight with them. If you're captured by them, throw up your hands and do as they say, but tell them, politely, no you're a pilot and fight differently from them. They're almost savage, so if they insist, you'd better be still.

No one will abort because of lack of oxygen. You'll be at 15,000 feet. If you get dizzy, go down under the bombers for a while. Over Russia we will be over 1,000 feet and below 6,000 feet. If your glass elbows break [gas line on wing drop-tanks], pull off to the side, have them fixed and catch us.

One more thing. If you've got to drink while you're there, for Christ's sake, don't get drunk. Be careful how you appear to the Russians with your crew chiefs. None of this 'okay, Joe' stuff. You treat Russian officers like brother officers – or rather, not like brother officers.

This whole thing is for show. That's why everything must be pansy. Cheers.

Crew chiefs and mechanics were taken on the mission to service the Mustangs in Russia, flying as gunners in the bombers. They were given brief instruction in aerial gunnery and were equipped with parachutes, dinghies, candy, cigarettes and toilet paper. At the appointed hour, all sixty-eight Mustangs (including a squadron from the 352nd Fighter Group) took off, assembled and set course for their destination. As the assemblage of bombers and fighters crossed the Polish border, they dropped their wing tanks. Near Warsaw, the bombers were attacked by about fifteen Bf 109s. Of the German fighters, five were shot down for the loss of one B-17. Jim Goodson's crew chief, Robert L. Gilbert, was flying as a waist gunner in the bomber, but baled out safely and later fought with a group of Russian guerrillas.

At 7.35 pm, the fighters arrived on course, on time, over the field at Piryatin near Poltava, where they landed spectacularly and were greeted with great enthusiasm by their Russian hosts. Blakeslee was immediately whisked away to make a radio broadcast in Moscow. Back at Piryatin, the vodka flowed on the longest night after the longest day of the Fourth Fighter Group. Deacon Hively acted as Blakeslee's deputy in the endless toasts and little ceremonies that marked the first night and day of their stay in Russia.

On the night of the second day, it was obvious that the Germans were well aware of the Fourth Fighter Group's visit to Russia, when a fleet of *Luftwaffe* bombers raided the Poltava airfield, destroying many of the American bombers and some of the Mustangs. The fighter pilots of the Fourth Fighter Group wanted to stage a retaliatory strike against the German airfield, but their Russian hosts would not allow it. 'You are our guest. We protect you. If you did this, Goebbels would say you had come to fight for us.'

After five days of Russian hospitality, the Debden P-51s had been duly serviced and prepared for the next leg of their historic flight. They left for Lucera air base near Foggia, Italy, escorting the bombers on the way in an attack on an oil refinery at Drohobycz, Poland. Fifteenth Air Force Mustangs rendezvoused with them near the Yugoslav coast and took over to provide withdrawal support for the bombers. While in Italy, it was arranged that the Fourth Fighter Group Mustangs would participate with those of the Fifteenth Air Force in a mission escorting bombers to targets in Budapest. However, about two-thirds of the Debden Mustang pilots were forced to abort when their engines began to malfunction. They were not equipped with the type of dust filters required in the Mediterranean area.

Blakeslee led the remaining P-51s, which had been given a 'roaming' assignment. When no German fighters appeared to harass the bombers, he was about to take the Mustangs down to look for targets of opportunity. Then Deacon Hively spotted between fifty and sixty Bf 109s approaching the bombers. This time the Debden fighters would be grossly outnumbered, but the German pilots chose to ignore the Mustangs and attack the bombers directly. Eight of the Bf 109s were shot down, including one by Hively, whose Mustang was then hit by a cannon shell that blew off his canopy and wounded his right eye. He briefly lost control of the aircraft, but recovered and, despite his eye wound and reduced vision in his other eye, managed to get back in the fight and shoot down two more Bf 109s. For this action he was awarded the Distinguished Service Cross.

When the Americans had landed again in Italy, after what was probably the last great dogfight of the war, Blakeslee discovered that four of his pilots, including Ralph 'Kid' Hofer, were missing. Captain Stanford and Lieutenant Norris were prisoners-of-war; Lieutenants Hofer and Sharp had been killed in action. On returning to Allied control, Stanford related the events surrounding the death of Hofer. On the way to Russia, Hofer and Stanford became separated during the air battle near Warsaw. Hofer lost contact with the group and landed at an airfield near Kiev. On the escort mission to Budapest, Stanford was leading No. 335 Fighter Squadron and Hofer was flying as his wingman. When they engaged the Bf 109s, Stanford attempted to drop his wing tanks and they failed to release. In the encounter, his over-straining engine threw a rod, causing him to withdraw from the action. Crippled, with oil covering his wind-screen, Stanford threw his P-51 into a spin to evade any enemy aircraft that might have followed him down in hopes of an easy kill. He assumed that Hofer, like a good wingman, had followed him down to protect him. Stanford crash-landed his Mustang in the hills near Budapest. He believed that the Mustang then buzzing him as he was ridding himself of his parachute pack was the Kid. He next saw and heard a Bf 109 tearing after that Mustang, firing as both aircraft crossed the field where he stood. The Mustang, presumably that of Hofer, crashed.

After several weeks the Germans reported, through the Red Cross, that the body of Ralph Hofer had been identified by his dog tags and had been buried in Hungary. The Kid was ultimately credited with the destruction of 30.5 enemy aircraft. He had been the first American flight officer in the European Theatre to qualify as an ace.

To most of the those at Debden, Blakeslee seemed indestructible. Not so, the vaunted *Luftwaffe*. In April 1944, the Fourth Fighter Group had destroyed 207 enemy aircraft, but in August, only 28. To Blakeslee, the end of the European war was practically in sight and he looked forward to setting up another Debden-like fighter group out in the Pacific, where the war with Japan still raged.

While the Fourth Fighter Group was still flying its P-47 Thunderbolts, Johnny Godfrey was going through a bleak period:

My next fifteen missions were frustrating ones. Not one Jerry did I bounce. Don [Gentile], meanwhile, shot three more, and Bob [Richards] shot one off my tail as our section was dive-bombing. In the group a fighting spirit was gaining momentum. Some of the older members finished their tours of operations and went back to the USA as instructors. Colonel Don quietly weeded out the undesirables, and now we had a real esprit de corps. I believe that some credit should be given to the younger members of the group, too. Pilots like Bob, Hofer, Megura and myself, and other comparative newcomers, had jolted the complacency of the more experienced pilots. We were showing them up, and they retaliated with their old vim and vigour. Bounces were made below 19,000 feet and some of them were dog-fighting on the deck. Colonel Don wasn't boasting when he said the Fourth would be the best fighter group in the Eighth Air Force.

Don Gentile recalled:

The time finally came for us in late February, 1944. There was no more need to put all our planes in the close support of the bombers. There was no more need to keep the formation at any cost. We were sent out there to go and get and clobber the Nazis. If they wouldn't come up into the air we would go down against their ground guns and shoot them up on the ground. Get them, that was the idea; kill them, trample them down.

It was this time I, personally, was ready for. I had been wanting to fly, and flying was practically my whole life. In the two years of mixing it with the Germans I had learned a great many things that you can't learn in any but the hard way. And there were many in Colonel Don Blakeslee's group who were in the same condition. It was no accident that when the bell finally rang for the big fight Colonel Blakeslee's team became, in seven weeks of the happiest, craziest hayriding ever, the highest-scoring outfit in the whole league.

From the diary of Lt Jack Raphael, 336th Fighter Squadron:

5 February 1944 – Early show to Beauvais-Paris area. Freelance group, but no Jerrys were up. Very little flak was thrown at us. Landed at Manston with my fuel gauge out. Beat up Manston and flew back to Debden on the deck. Got reported for beating up Manston and caught hell, also a week as airfield controller! Justice – BAH!

Blakeslee was famously quoted in the New York press as saying, 'Fighter pilots and women don't mix.' It enraged the wives and girl friends of fighter pilots throughout America. At Debden, his fliers were known as 'Blakeslee's Bachelors'. By the time he returned to England and the base, he was being quoted as saying, 'You can't fight the war without 'em.'

It soon transpired that, while in the States he had secretly married his hometown girl. More than anything, he wanted to continue to fly combat missions with his fellow pilots of the Fourth Fighter Group, but it was not to be. He was eventually told that he was too valuable to risk on further flights over Germany. He was to be relieved of command at Debden and returned to the Zone of the Interior and a desk job. It was a consolation of a sort that his great rival in the race for the top-scoring fighter group of the Eighth Air Force, Hub Zemke, was also being taken off ops. Until their orders came through, though, both Zemke and Blakeslee were permitted to continue flying missions with their groups.

The day before Colonel Zemke was due to report to the 65th Fighter Wing for his new job, he went on what was to be his last mission. Over Germany, his Mustang iced up in cloud and became uncontrollable. He was forced to bale out and became a prisoner-of-war. As soon as that information reached Wing headquarters, Blakeslee received a phone call from General Jesse Auton, the 65th Fighter Wing commander, telling him that he was grounded, effective immediately.

In the days that followed, as he awaited his posting, Don Blakeslee had time to reflect on his time at Debden and leading the Fourth Fighter Group. He made a flight down to his old RAF base, Biggin Hill, where he now found only a few of the British officers he had known years before. Of the 150 pilots that had sailed with him to England, only three were still around. Then the day came when he left the Debden base for the last time. 'You all know how I feel about leaving . . .', was about all he could manage. He would miss them and they him.

From the diary of Lt Jack Raphael, 336th Fighter Squadron:

28 February 1944 – Some of the fellows went on the first Mustang show. Garrison, Megura, 'Pappy' Smith and Beeson shot down a Ju 88 trying to take off from his field. Fraser crashed on the field and burned. Killed instantly. Got my old Thunderbolt, VF-M, taken from me and got a new P-51B-5 Mustang, VF-N. George and I went to the darkroom, developed a couple of rolls of film and made enlargements until midnight. Didn't get to bed until 1:00 am.

CHAPTER NINE

Little Friends

From the diary of Lt Jack Raphael, 336th Fighter Squadron:

> 31 January 1944 – Squadron split in two for show today. Half as dive-bombers and half as fighter escort. Bombed Gilze-Rijen air-drome in Holland. Gentile and I blew up the fuel dump. 30+ Me 109s over us during the bombing, but cover did a fine job and shot down six. Garrison, Carlson, Clotfelter, Ellington, Sobanski and Beeson were the killers. Weather bad on return, not too much flak, just enough to make things interesting. Spent the evening in the mess. Had a few drinks to celebrate the good show.

Not long after receiving their Mustangs, the speculation among the pilots of the Fourth Fighter Group had focused on when they would be sent on the historic first mission to Berlin, – 'Big B' as the pilots referred to it. The Eighth Air Force had scheduled, and then cancelled, that mission six times during February 1944. It was finally set for 3 March. The bombers and fighters took off, assembled and were under way to the Continent, when deteriorating weather conditions caused their recall.

The Fourth Fighter Group was leading the escorting fighter force and its aircraft were to be the first American fighters to penetrate the airspace of the German capital. With the recall of the bombers, the fighters were also ordered to return to base, but, among the many 'bugs' that were plaguing the early Mustangs of the Eighth Air Force, radio malfunction was widespread during this mission. Many of the fighter pilots therefore failed to hear the recall order from Colonel Blakeslee. While half of No. 336th Squadron had turned back for Debden, the other eight pilots continued through the cloud build-up. When they emerged, they immediately ran into approximately sixty enemy fighter aircraft. It was not possible for wingmen to stay with their leaders in the situation. Most of the American pilots found themselves on the defensive and had to struggle to regain an equal footing with their adversaries.

Johnny Godfrey recalled:

I freed myself from the first mad onslaught and headed for the deck. I heard some of the other boys on the R/T trying to re-form. I felt more secure in the knowledge that some of them had escaped also. I started climbing back to see if I could spot them. At 28,000 feet I levelled off without seeing a plane in the sky. Calling on the R/T for their positions, I failed to receive any answer. A plane was approaching, and because of its long nose I thought it was a Mustang. Turning into it I received a shock; it was neither a Mustang nor an Me 109, but a new Focke-Wulf; its long nose was the latest improvement of the famed Fw. These planes with the longer noses were rumoured to have more horsepower than their predecessors, and were capable of giving a Mustang a rough time. We met practically head-on and both of us banked our planes in preparation for a dogfight.

Around and around we went. Sometimes the Fw got in close, and other times, when I'd drop my flap to tighten my turn, I was in a position to fire; but the German, sensing my superior position, kept swinging down in the turn, gaining speed and quickly pulling up, and with the advantage he would then pour down on my tail. Time was in his favour; he could fight that way for an hour and still have enough fuel to land anywhere below him. I still had 400 miles of enemy territory to fly over before I could land. Something had to be done. Throwing caution to the wind I lifted a flap, dove and pulled up in a steep turn, at the same time dropping a little flap. The G was terrific, but it worked, and I had the Jerry nailed for sure. Pressing the tit I waited, but nothing happened, not a damned thing. My guns weren't firing.

By taking this last gamble I had lost altitude but had been able to bring my guns to bear while flying below the Fw. With his advantage of height he came down, pulled up sharp, and was smack-dab on my tail again. The 20 mm cannon belched and I could see what looked like golf balls streaming by me. A little less deflection and those seemingly harmless golf balls would have exploded instantly upon contact with my plane.

'Never turn your back on an enemy' was a byword with us, but I had no choice. Turning the plane over on its back I yanked the stick to my gut. My throttle was wide open and I left it there as I dove. The needle stopped at 600 miles per hour – that was as far as it could go on the dial. Pulling out I expected at any minute to have the wings rip off, the plane was bucking so much. The last part of my pull-up brought me up into clouds. I was thankful to have evaded the long-nosed Fw, for that pilot was undoubtedly the best that I had ever met. I saw no other planes on the way home and had to wait until landing to hear the fate of my buddies.

Don Gentile also recalled the mission:

A group of Me 110s, Do 217s and Ju 88s passed underneath us coming head-on. I rolled over starboard and started down but was bounced by ten Fw 190s, which Lt Millikan, doing an outstanding job, engaged and drove away from me. I dove on down and got on the tail of a twin-engined plane, but my canopy was so badly frosted over that I couldn't see anything. I was scared of hitting him so pulled up and turned my defroster on and when the canopy started to clear there was a 110 right beside me and firing at me. I broke away and was again bounced by three Fw 190s. I turned into them, met them head-on and they just kept going. I then bounced the Do 217 in a port turn, fired a short burst above and astern, and my gunsight went out. I pulled up, gave another short burst and saw strikes. Just then two 190s flashed past, one on each side so I pulled away.

I asked Lt Millikan if he was with me and he said 'Hell, I'm fighting ten Fws,' so I figured he needed help. I tried to gather the odd Mustang I saw floating around telling him to join up. Then I saw a gaggle beneath me going around in a pretty good formation. I half-rolled and went down, but suddenly found myself in the midst of twelve to fourteen 190s, with no Mustangs around. I did a port, steep climb turn full bore. On the way up an Fw 190 was in front of me. I pulled around and put him under my nose and fired a burst. I then repeated the process, saw some pieces come off and the pilot bale out.

In the encounter, Don scored two enemy aircraft destroyed. 'Swede' Carlson, Vermont Garrison and Willard Millikan each claimed an Me 110 shot down and Garrison also downed an Fw 190. Lieutenant Glenn Herter was downed in the action. Lieutenant Philip Dunn got lost on the way back to England and ran out of fuel. He became a prisoner-of-war. Garrison's Mustang was hit by flak near Boulogne, France, and he too was taken prisoner.

On 6 March a force of 730 B-17s and B-24s returned to Berlin in the company of 803 little friends from both Eighth and Ninth Fighter Commands. They had been told it would be a rough mission. The weather was once again terrible over the target and the enemy fighter opposition was ferocious. Intense cloud cover meant that the bombers were unable to attack their primary industrial targets in the suburbs of the city. Ultimately, the bombing results were poor.

The bomber stream was approaching Berlin accompanied by the Mustangs of the Fourth Fighter Group. The *Luftwaffe* fighters attacked the American heavies, queuing up to roll through the bomber formations and then repeat their attacks. Lieutenant Nick 'Cowboy' Megura of the Fourth Fighter Group spotted over twenty single-engined enemy aircraft 6,000 feet below him. The enemy aircraft were evidently providing cover for at least twenty more rocket-laden twin-engined planes. Megura and other Mustang pilots dived on the Germans. He focused on three Me 110 rocket-carriers, which split their formation and fled without firing their missiles. Then he spotted three more Me 110s, which had just fired their rockets into the bomber formations. The German aircraft were in tight formation, making an unusually good target for the American, who fired, covering the three enemy aircraft with strikes. He noted his bullets hitting the cockpit and both engines of the nearest German aircraft. Concentrating on the second aircraft, Megura fired again and the target exploded and slid into an unrecoverable dive, streaming black smoke. The Mustang pilot then pursued the remaining German twin to near ground level, where he found that only one of his six .50 calibre machine-guns was still working. He closed on the enemy aircraft and fired, hitting the cockpit and the port engine. He followed it for a short while and watched as it crashed near an aerodrome. His ammunition exhausted, Megura set course for Debden.

Another eventful day for the Fourth Fighter Group was 29 March. The target of the bombers was Brunswick, Germany, and the Mustang pilots encountered heavy enemy fighter opposition on the way. It came at them from two directions, requiring the Americans to split into two groups to attack the enemy aircraft.

Flying as Blue 1 in Shirtblue Squadron, Don Gentile led his Mustangs below the bomber stream in a bounce on seven or eight Fw 190s at 18,000 feet. He positioned his aircraft, which he had named *Shangri-la*, behind one of the Fw 190s, fired and saw strikes around the German's cockpit. Slowly, the Fw 190 rolled over into a vertical dive. Almost immediately, Don heard Johnny Godfrey yell 'Break' as he spotted two Fw 190s on Don's tail. Don broke hard left and the G forces briefly caused him to black out. Recovering, he realised that a Fw 190 was nicely placed 300 yards in front of him. Firing quickly, his bullets caused the enemy pilot to bale out.

Johnny was following Don down when his engine suddenly cut out. He had neglected to switch his fuel selector valve. Quickly doing so, he then sighted five Focke-Wulfs being chased by two Mustangs and joined in the chase. He noticed one of the German pilots baling out. As the little string of Fws and P-51s neared the deck, Johnny was finally able to line up on one of the enemy aircraft, giving it a half dozen short bursts, which caused it to blow up at ground level. In seconds, he was on the tail of a second Fw, peppering it with strikes and sending it down in a trail of heavy black smoke.

Regrouping, the Mustangs began a gentle climbing turn and soon encountered a Heinkel He 111 bomber crossing their course. Johnny had position on the German and fired, observing several strikes. Fred Glover then added to the attack, exhausting his ammunition into the enemy bomber, which crash-landed in a meadow.

Now joined by another Mustang, Don was jumped by two Bf 109s. He called for the other Mustang pilot to break, but his transmission was not heard. He soon got into position with the two Germans and chased them into cloud. He then sighted another Bf 109 following him. He broke and reversed his turn to end up behind this latest Messerschmitt. He took a shot and glycol immediately began to stream from the enemy fighter. The pilot baled out.

As well as having a good partnership in the air, Johnny Godfrey and Don Gentile were becoming great friends on the ground. Johnny recalled:

Don and I were fast becoming good friends, not only in the air, but on the ground. His roommate had baled out over Germany [actually, Steve Pisanos had crash-landed his Mustang in France during the Bordeaux mission of 5 March 1944]. Both of us had lost our buddies, and we spent more and more time in each other's company. I didn't want to leave my room and Don was very happy in his; for that reason we didn't bunk together. My new roommate was Lieutenant Robert S. Tussey, from Altoona, Pennsylvania. Robert had joined the squadron a month before and was already showing promise of being a good fighter pilot, having shot down two Jerries the previous week.

From the diary of Lt Jack Raphael, 336th Fighter Squadron:

8 March 1944 – Show to Berlin. Started, but both wing tanks were leaking, so had to return. Group got 16, but Sel Edner missing. Gentile got 3; Godfrey 2 and Tussey bagged a Ju 88. Spent all

afternoon and most of the evening in the darkroom making another batch of enlargements. Went to the mess for a short time and then headed for the room about 11:00 pm.

12 March 1944 – Got my escape pictures taken during the morning, but didn't do much else. Got a new plane assigned to me and worked on it during the afternoon. Made a couple of enlargements and then got cleaned up before dinner. Got inebriated on the squadron doctor's orders during the evening.

Late in March, the Mustangs of the Fourth Fighter Group were re-painted with bright red noses and the paint scheme was soon well known by both the Allies and the Germans. In addition to the nose red, Johnny and Don both had their cowling panels painted in a red-and-white checkerboard pattern to improve recognition for each other. The P-47 Thunderbolts of Hub Zemke's 56th Fighter Group were the first group in Eighth Fighter Command to distinguish their planes with an identifying nose colour. They painted the nosebands of the aircraft of each squadron with a different colour. Soon, Eighth Fighter Command decided to standardise the nose markings of the fighters of each group in a system that would make them all easily identifiable in the air.

With the coming of spring, Eighth Bomber Command was striking targets at ever-greater distances from England, testing the capabilities of Eighth Fighter Command. The German flak defences were being beefed-up around the more sensitive targets while, at the same time, fewer and fewer *Luftwaffe* fighters were rising to meet the Allied Thunderbolts and Mustangs.

With these changes, it was incumbent upon Eighth Fighter Command to rethink its tactics. As its fighter strength increased with the arrival of many new Mustangs, the Command was able to send more of its fighters down to the deck to locate and destroy enemy aircraft on their airfields, while the rest of the Allied fighter force stayed up protecting the bombers. With equal credit now given for the destruction of enemy aircraft on the ground and in the air, this would quickly add to the scores of many American fighter pilots. However, it would also expose them to the worst odds of the air war. The strafing attacks on the German aerodromes carried with them the most dangerous threat – intense and accurate flak. The danger was especially great for the pilots of the Mustangs, with their highly vulnerable underslung radiators.

Among the highest achievers of the new tactic was Major Jim Goodson of the 336th Squadron, who became known as the 'King of the Strafers'. The new-type offence was introduced on 5 April, when eleven Eighth Fighter Command groups were ordered to attack various *Luftwaffe* airfields. Once again, the weather played a major part in the operation and only three of the fighter groups were able to complete the mission. Hitting several airfields around Berlin, the pilots of the Fourth Fighter Group achieved good results. Goodson led the 336th Squadron in a strike on the Stendal aerodrome, which resulted in more than twenty-five enemy aircraft being destroyed on the ground. Fortunately for the Fourth Fighter Group, very little flak was encountered in this attack. Unfortunately for the pilots of the 334th Squadron, of four Mustangs attacking an airfield near Brandenburg, two were shot down by ground fire. One of the Mustangs shot down was that of the squadron's highest-scoring ace (also Don Gentile's principal rival in the ace race), Duane Beeson, who became a prisoner-of-war.

From the diary of Lt Jack Raphael, 336th Fighter Squadron:

> 15 March 1944 – Loafed around dispersal and read intelligence reports all morning. Spent the entire afternoon sanding down and polishing my new plane. 4th Group got red noses painted on our Mustangs. Looks good! After supper, came back to the room to write a letter before having a late snack.

On 8 April the target was Brunswick again. The place had a reputation among both bomber and fighter pilots of the Eighth Air Force for putting up the fiercest flak and fighter resistance of any target. Don Gentile was leading Shirtblue Squadron and as the Fourth Fighter Group neared its rendezvous point with the bombers, Colonel Blakeslee called: 'Horseback to all Horseback aircraft. 100-plus approaching bombers at 11 o'clock.'

The masses of German fighters had been brilliantly vectored to the American bombers and waited for them up-sun. The Fourth Fighter Group had been assigned to shepherd B-24 Liberators this day and, as they watched, dozens of enemy fighters fell on the bombers, plunging through their combat box defensive formations. In the first pass, six of the B-24s began the long fall, knocked from the bomber stream by the intense fire of the German fighters. The gunners in the bombers were putting up a good fight and scoring hits on many of the attacking aircraft, but they desperately needed help. It came quickly in the form of several Mustangs led by Gentile, Millikan, and Red Dog Norley, all squaring off against the enemy aircraft as they emerged beneath the bomber stream.

For a while it seemed to be Norley's show. He aligned a deflection shot on a Bf 109 at a range of about 300 yards and shot it out of the sky. Turning, he sighted an Fw 190 2,000 feet below him and gave chase. He forced the German into a tight climbing turn to port and, just before he would have overshot the Fw 190, he used twenty degrees of flap to slow his Mustang. He was able to out-turn the enemy aircraft, which then rolled over into a steep dive. The enemy pilot couldn't escape the attentions of Red Dog, however, and soon became his second victim of the battle. Norley's windscreen was covered with oil from the smoking Fw. Climbing away from that action, his windscreen began to clear and he spotted another Fw 190 coming down to engage him. Norley subtly evaded the German pilot and out-turned him, gaining the advantage. He then chased the Fw 190 down for more than a mile and got within firing range. He used only a few short bursts and the canopy came off this next victim as the Focke-Wulf went end over end into cloud. Next, as he again began climbing, Red Dog noticed another Fw 190 descending towards him in what appeared to be a gentle glide. It seemed to him that the German had probably been hit while diving through the bomber formations. The adversaries began a tail-chase and the Focke-Wulf pilot out-turned Norley. They were coming at each other head-on when the German did a split-S and headed for the deck with Norley in hot pursuit. As they pulled out of the dive, Norley blacked out and came to in a climb at 4,000 feet. He searched frantically for the enemy aircraft and finally saw its wreckage burning on the ground off to his left. Norley's score for the day was three.

Don Gentile, meanwhile, brought his Mustangs into combat with a mixture of thirty Fw 190s and Bf 109s. Several of the German pilots decided to leave the area rather than tangle with the red-nosed P-51s. He was targeting a Fw 190 at 16,000 feet when he was bounced by three Fw 190s, forcing him to break off the chase. But he soon found another Fw 190 and dispatched it. To his 2 o'clock position Don saw an Fw clobbering a Mustang and raced to help the hapless American pilot. Before he could get there, however, the Mustang was ablaze. He engaged the German pilot and they chased each other down from 22,000 to 8,000 feet, with the German throttling back and causing Don to over-shoot him, followed by Don out-turning him. In the end, Don prevailed and the enemy pilot baled out. He searched for another victim and found a third Fw 190 down among the treetops. But this man was a superb flyer – well above the average. For more than ten minutes the two fighters duelled just over the trees and into the ravines. Then, Don overshot the German, but help appeared instantly when Pierce McKennon arrived to blast the Fw 190, sending it into the trees with its pilot.

Don returned to Debden with three more enemy aircraft to his credit and was elated when he landed and climbed out of *Shangri-la* after doing a few victory rolls over the field at little more than 100 feet. His score for the past thirty days alone was eighteen. It was a spectacular performance among a stellar one by the whole group. The Fourth Fighter Group had shot down thirty-one enemy aircraft for the loss of just four Mustangs. Grover Hall recalled:

> How . . . to explain the 31–4 battle? The Germans had had every advantage: they were over their own country and they outnumbered the 4th's Mustangs. Without indulging in any *alma mater* lapse, I submit that the answer is entirely obvious and unquestionable. Simply: the American pilots excelled the German pilots in combat prowess.
>
> The 4th had destroyed 76 aircraft in the first eight days of April. The 4th was at the summit of its power. The Germans knew and talked of the 'red nose boys'. The name of the 4th was called blessed by the bomber groups: not infrequently they phoned Blakeslee after a mission to express admiration and gratitude for the way the 4th had stomped on Huns attacking the bombers.

In April, the newspaper-wire service-radio spin machine was operating at 'full military power' on the Debden base. The pilots were very close to exceeding the total of enemy aircraft destroyed by the rival 56th Fighter Group. They had a realistic expectation of surpassing the 500-destroyed mark by the end of the month, with luck and the co-operation of the weather and the *Luftwaffe*. Morale was high. Since being equipped with the P-51 Mustang, the fortunes of the group had, in general, risen considerably and those of a few, including Don and Johnny, substantially . . . but at a price.

Ira Wolfert, a reporter for the North American Newspaper *Alliance* wanted to do a series of in-depth articles about Don. Don agreed and Wolfert moved in with him, occupying the bunk that Steve Pisanos had used before being forced down in France. From their first hours together, Wolfert was aware of the strain that Gentile was under. He asked Don: 'Now that you've got 27, have you thought of taking a rest? You've used up a lot of your luck.' Don replied:

> Yeah, I know. I've been thinking about Beeson. But this war is my chance. I don't want to go back after the war and pilot an airliner between New York and Cincinnati. I want to come out of it with more planes destroyed than anybody else. That's been my plan for some time. That's the reason I don't go to London and save my money. Rickenbacker got his chance that way in the other war.

'You've had some close calls lately,' said Wolfert. 'Yeah, but unless the flak gets me, I can make it. I'm gonna make a couple more shows and take a rest,' said Don.

Grover Hall recalled:

> But the strain of the inner debate was perceptible in Gentile's face. He
> was weighing every angle: How much longer could he beat the game?
> He was tired physically and his brain was addled, and that made him
> sag physically.

Don had long since completed his tour of duty. He had later requested
and been granted three extensions of his tour. Finally, the War Department decided that Gentile should be removed from combat status and
returned to the United States to participate in a series of war bond rallies
and personal appearances.

The 336th Squadron's medical officer's job included keeping a watchful
eye on the squadron's pilots for any signs of nervous strain, which he
referred to as 'the shakes'. Following the mission of 5 April, he suggested
that Johnny Godfrey take seven days' leave to rest and relax after his
lengthy stretch of combat flying. Johnny recalled:

> He had been watching me for some time. The twitching about my
> eyes and mouth was now quite noticeable and my hands trembled.
> It was nothing serious if caught in time. A week's rest away from
> the base, away from its tense excitement, was what the doctor
> recommended. If I would like to spend my time in a 'flak' home,
> arrangements would be made. That wasn't for me; most of the boys
> there were from bomber crews, who suffered more from the shakes
> than fighter pilots. They were the ones who had nicknamed the rest
> home.

Instead, Johnny packed his bag and caught the 5.15 pm train from
Audley End for London. He checked in at the Prince's Garden Club and
talked for a while with Mrs C, who tactfully refrained from mentioning
Bob Richards' death. Then he set out for some R and R in London. He
recalled:

> Have you ever spent some time at a place where every minute was
> filled with joy, where even the air seemed different and exciting – then
> return later to the same place to find that everything has changed?
> Actually, it hadn't changed – it was probably the same but your
> perspective had altered so that now everything seemed drab and dull.
> That was my reaction. The same bars were jammed with people, but
> the faces were those of strangers. The war had taken its toll, and the

boys whom I had trained and flown with were few and far between. The girls seemed old, and the few I did meet who I recognised had no appeal for me now. Even the drinks didn't taste the same, and regardless of how many I downed I couldn't recapture what it was I was looking for. Disgustedly, I walked alone through the dark streets from Piccadilly to the Prince's Garden Club.

From the diary of Lt Jack Raphael, 336th Fighter Squadron:

23 March 1944 – Still non-operational. Show to Brunswick. Godfrey got an Me 109, Goody got 2 and Gentile got 2. Flew the Fairchild for an hour during the afternoon. Had an eye examination. Went to a photo club meeting after supper and adjourned to the darkroom for a short time. Had something to eat then called it a day.

The combat exploits of Godfrey, and especially Gentile, had continued to feed the international publicity machine. In April 1944, when Don's score reached thirty, the press were insatiable in their desire to make maximum capital from his combat exploits. Grover Hall recounted:

. . . General Doolittle's headquarters had directed me, the Debden public relations officer, to delay the announcement. Seven of Gentile's 30 were destroyed on the ground. At the time there was a burgeoning controversy and confusion over whether parked aircraft should be counted the same as those bagged in aerial combat, though everybody recognised that ground-strafing was far more hazardous than air-fighting. Doolittle's headquarters, whose PRO section was commendably conscientious, did not want to make the distinction between ground and air kills. It wanted to let the newspapers themselves decide how to treat the difference. It was decided that a simple communiqué would be made to the effect that Gentile had destroyed so many in the air and so many on the ground.

Hall was then directed by Eighth Air Force headquarters to refrain from any announcement of Gentile's achievement for a few days, until the Air Force claims board had done its work of assessing and officially confirming Don's claims. Correspondent Ira Wolfert was well aware of the circumstances and agreed to cooperate with the Air Force and withhold his own story of Gentile, until the Air Force approved a release date. In the end, however, whether accidentally or intentionally, another wire service jumped the gun, releasing the story early. Grover Hall recalled:

. . . the fat was now in the fire. Gentile was a national figure. He was hailed throughout the Zone of the Interior as the 'ace of aces'. From this morning forward, Gentile was destined to be machine-gunned by photographers, shadowed by newsreel cameramen, bound by reporters and gagged with microphones.

International News Service then cabled the following to US newspapers:

AN EIGHTH AIR FORCE FIGHTER STATION, ENGLAND, April 10 – (INS) – Col Don Blakeslee's 4th Fighter Group today broke all records for the European Theater of Operations, boosting their score to 403 in a strafing mission over France. The colorful, hard-flying group swept into first place in the fighter sweep-stakes, gaining the triple-tiered crown for having the highest scoring group, the No. 1 ace, Capt. Don Gentile, and the record for 31 kills in a single mission.

There followed a visit to Debden by General Eisenhower, Supreme Allied Commander of the Allied Expeditionary Forces; General Carl Spaatz, Commander US Strategic Air Forces, Europe; Lieutenant General James A. Doolittle, Commander, Eighth Air Force; Major-General William Kepner, Commander, Eighth Fighter Command; and Brigadier General Jesse Auton, Commander, 65th Fighter Wing, along with a great number of press photographers and reporters. *The New York Times* wrote:

A UNITED STATES FIGHTER BASE, ENGLAND – (AP) – Fourth Fighter Group pilots were told today by Gen. Eisenhower that their role in the great three-way invasion of Europe soon would be flying a dawn-to-dusk death express against the German Air Force . . .
    Gen. Eisenhower said he had a feeling of great privilege and almost humility in visiting such a group of fighting men as the 4th . . .

It was on this occasion that Eisenhower met and said to Don Gentile: 'You seem to be a one-man air force.'
Grover Hall recalled:

There was whimsy in this. AAF headquarters had done all things to discourage the idea of individual performance and to encourage the idea of team-work. In a few hours all the cadets in America would be reading that the Supreme Commander had called Gentile a 'one man air force'.

Highballs and wine were served in the Officers' Mess before lunch. Eisenhower told the pilots they could have anything they wanted, because Washington was giving him everything he asked for. It was mentioned that they would prefer their operational whiskey to be bourbon instead of Scotch. From then on, it was bourbon or rye (plus the stuff labelled Spiritous Frumenti, which may have been anything).

Now Don had come to a point where he agreed to go back to the United States for a month and participate in war bond rallies and public relations activities, but only on the condition that he then be allowed to return to fly combat missions with the group. It was in this period, while he was awaiting orders for his leave, that a strange event occurred. Newsreel cameramen continued to haunt the base and, on 13 April, they had approached Don to ask for his cooperation in some filming they wanted to do when the group returned from their mission that day. They asked him to come in very low so that they could get some good shots of him buzzing the field.

On the mission, the Fourth Fighter Group flew near Schweinfurt, Germany, when it got into combat with a contingent of enemy fighters. Don realised that these were relatively inexperienced German pilots who were making easy targets of themselves with their naive tactics and inept manoeuvres. He attacked and then noticed a Mustang below him being clobbered by an Fw 190. He broke off his action on the enemy aircraft and dived to the aid of the Mustang pilot. On the return trip to Debden, he remembered the newsreel cameramen waiting at his dispersal on the airfield. Approaching the base, he decided to give the press guys something special to shoot. The mission that day, he knew, would be his last for a while and the last opportunity for such a buzz job for a long time. He had been in the air for more than six hours and must have been tired. He brought *Shangri-la* down to treetop level on the run-in and then lower still as he flashed down the main runway.

Grover Hall recalled:

We saw the red nose of Gentile's Mustang come whipping across the field towards us. He was perhaps 25 feet high. There is a rise in the field. For a moment the plane was lost to view behind it. Then its red nose showed again against the green. He was low enough to smack the camera over. We thought: 'When's he going to pull up?'

'He was coming in low,' the Associated Press said later, 'after a seven-hour flight when his plane lost power.'

That was a charitable way to explain it. Truth was, Gentile had not circled enough on the deck to regain his depth perception. The plane mushed. It struck the grass field wheels up about 100 yards in front of the crowd, members of which hit the ground or jumped into ditches. The plane banged the ground and appeared to bounce.

Onlookers gasped as the Mustang leap-frogged over their heads, prop windmilling, the blades bent like lily petals. Blakeslee saw it from a distance and cursed.

Gentile realised he was going to crash, and his reflexes rushed ahead to take charge until his thoughts could catch up. He cut switches right and left to preclude a contact explosion . . . He saw his airspeed falling and picked out the likeliest spot for a crash-landing. He braced his feet and hands to keep from bashing his face as the ship struck just short of a ditch and a high-tension line.

'Look at him!' exclaimed the first to sight Gentile. He was sitting on the wing of his Mustang, reflecting gloomily on the destruction of his beautiful ship, which he had thought of taking back home for use in bond-selling. The Mustang had a cracked back; it looked like a shrimp. Gentile only had a bruised shoulder and sore finger.

Colonel Blakeslee was fuming. He had long since made it clear that any pilot who damaged a plane while buzzing would never again be allowed to fly combat for the Fourth Fighter Group. Don was grounded. [Anxious to know if his promotion had come through, Gentile later wrote to Colonel Blakeslee. The colonel informed Don that his promotion had bounced because he had failed to demonstrate appropriate remorse in his explanation to General Auton as to how he had managed to prang his Mustang, when buzzing the airfield after the Group's mission on 13 April to Schweinfurt. It mattered little. Gentile would not be returning to Debden or flying combat missions again.]

Eighth Fighter Command was growing, with the formation of more fighter groups and the arrival of many new Mustangs and American-trained pilots. The command now had the relative luxury of assigning certain groups to roles other than escorting the bombers. On 22 April, the Fourth Fighter Group was operating at 12,000 feet, looking for German fighters. Johnny, who was flying next to Colonel Blakeslee, sighted a very large formation of what appeared to be enemy fighters well below them to their 2 o'clock position. He alerted Blakeslee who called his pilots:

This is Horseback here. Johnny's right. I want no plane – I repeat – no plane to attack by himself. We have a perfect bounce. 336 and 335 will let down following me. 334 stay around 5,000 feet to give us cover. If no more Jerries come in on us, you will be free to come down.

Thirty-two red-nosed P-51s then entered a shallow diving turn. When they emerged from it, they were perfectly positioned behind a mass of forty Fw 190s and Bf 109s. From the start it was a mêlée. Johnny was flying with a new wingman. Early in the battle he had been finding it impossible to take a shot when he was in position behind an enemy plane, as his wingman continually yelled for him to break. Some of the German pilots had gone into a Lufberry [a First World War defensive tactic] circle and Johnny could not align on one. He broke away and climbed to get away from the circle, his wingman staying firmly with him. Then one of the Bf 109s swung wide, presenting himself to Johnny, who quickly set up a 30-degree deflection shot, which made the engine of the Messerschmitt blaze. The victim plunged earthward, trailing fiery smoke.

Pulling up and away from the central action again, Johnny spotted another enemy fighter wide of the bunch. Though more difficult to align on than his first kill, this Bf 109 too was soon aflame and heading down. Johnny caught sight of yet another Bf 109 immediately above him, which was apparently trying to leave the action and get down to ground level. Johnny chased him over the treetops and fired, witnessing hits on the tail and then up around the cockpit. He must have killed the enemy pilot, for the engine of the Messerschmitt seemed to be running normally as the aircraft slipped off on one wing and tore into the trees. Having chalked up three kills in a short time, Johnny turned and climbed to locate the main battle again, but his pursuit of the last German had carried him well away from it. Then he heard Blakeslee order the group back to Debden.

Don Gentile was waiting at the 336th dispersal when Johnny taxied *Reggie's Reply* into his revetment. 'Bags of Huns, bags of Huns!' yelled Johnny. 'How many did you get?' Don asked. 'Three,' Johnny replied. Don had just learned that his orders to return to the US for a month had been issued. He would soon be leaving Debden and air combat. Hearing the results now of the day's action in the group (Norley – two, Godfrey – three, Millikan – four), he was clearly having second thoughts about leaving. 'Gee, save me some, will you, fellas?' said Don.

When he was completing his combat report, Johnny received a phone call from Gibby, JJ's friend at the 356th Fighter Group, informing him that JJ's plane had been badly shot up. In their mission that day, JJ had destroyed an Fw 190 and a Ju 88, but had been hit in the cockpit by a

20 mm cannon shell, severely injuring one leg. He had managed to apply a tourniquet and bring his aircraft back to the Martlesham base. JJ was then in surgery at the Diss Hospital.

The 25th was a fine spring day and Johnny decided to take Lucky with him when he flew up to see JJ. After strapping in, his crew chief handed the dog to him. Sitting Lucky on his knee, Johnny tied the leash to his harness strap and they were off. Lucky had spent so much time out at the 336th Squadron dispersal that he was used to the loud engine noise and wasn't phased by his first ride in a Mustang. They landed at the American bomber base a few miles from the hospital. Walking into the ward, Johnny put Lucky down and the dog jumped onto JJ's bed and licked his hands. Johnny was saddened to see his old friend, who was now out of the war and soon to be evacuated to the US. He couldn't help wondering, after the loss of Bob Richards and now the serious injury of JJ, how much longer it would be before his own combat luck would run out.

He needn't have worried. Within days he heard from both the adjutant and Grover Hall that he was being promoted to captain and was shortly to meet Don Gentile at Chorley in Lancashire. They would both be returning to the US on a public relations tour for a month. Being honest with himself, Johnny had to admit that his earlier quest to avenge the death of his brother Reggie had since been replaced by a powerful desire to become the top-scoring fighter pilot of the war. There at Debden, he was at the height of his performance as a fighter pilot. He had destroyed twenty-nine enemy planes and his recent success rate seemed to indicate that he could increase that figure to at least fifty before the war ended. But he was being removed, at least temporarily, from the fight. He shared Don's mixed feelings about being sent back to America at what they both saw as such an important moment in their careers as fighter pilots.

Johnny said his goodbyes to his many friends at Debden, to Mrs C in London and to his nurse friend, Charlotte Fredericks, promising to keep in touch with her. The next day he packed, grabbed Lucky and climbed into a twin-engined Oxford transport that would fly him to meet Don at Chorley. Before leaving the area, the pilot considerately circled the field at Debden allowing Johnny a last look at the base that had meant so much to him.

At Chorley, Johnny walked into the room where Don was waiting. Don greeted him:

Hi, Johnny, I've been expecting you. They called me from London yesterday and gave me the scoop. It sounds like a good deal from the outline Public Relations gave me. We're leaving here tomorrow, according to the scuttlebutt I heard, so don't bother to unpack.

The next morning they left for Greenock, Scotland, to board the *Ile de France* for the voyage to the US. Lucky was smuggled aboard ship, carefully wrapped in Johnny's raincoat. All went well for most of the six-day journey, but eventually the dog was discovered and the boat commander notified. He ordered Johnny to either shoot Lucky or throw him overboard, because no pets would be allowed to disembark from the ship. Johnny did not intend to obey the order and enlisted the help of a friendly steward who offered to get Lucky off the ship and board him at a pet shop in New York until Johnny could pick him up. When the ship pulled into New York harbour, the boat commander came to Don and Johnny's room and searched it. Not finding the dog, and getting no co-operation and plenty of insolence from Johnny, he threatened him with a court martial.

Don and Johnny were flown immediately to Washington for a briefing at the Pentagon by US Army Air Forces Public Relations personnel. Wherever they were taken in the US, they were to be billed as the top Air Force ace and the top wingman. Teamwork was to be their basic theme and, no matter what questions were asked of them, they were not to mention individual combat. A legend had been created around them, beginning with that particular Berlin mission in which he and Don had shot down five planes. However, the fact was that, of the thirty enemy planes that Don had destroyed, Johnny had actually only helped in the destruction of ten.

Then the pair was ushered into the office of 'Hap' Arnold, commanding general of the Air Force. Johnny recalled the meeting:

Here was the brains behind the United States Army Air Force. The general's manner was unassuming and cordial. We sat for half an hour as he questioned us concerning the aerial battles over Germany. For one so far removed from the battlefield his knowledge was amazing. He listened intently, as we offered comparisons of German and American planes. We told him nothing, probably, which he didn't already know, but the way he listened filled us with great respect for him.

Finally, the boys were taken to their rooms at the Bolling Field officers' quarters. It was their first opportunity to phone their parents. The Air Force had notified their families of their return and invited them down to join the boys. A large press conference had been laid on the next day and in the morning the newspapers reported their arrival with headlines like: 'Captains Courageous', 'The Damon and Pythias of the Air Force' and 'The Greatest Team in Air Force History'. A luncheon was arranged for them at the Senate Building, where Don and Johnny were sponsored by Senators Taft and Green of Ohio and Rhode Island respectively. Johnny recalled:

> Senator Lehman of New York had a cold and was unable to attend the luncheon; but later we went to his apartment and gave him his son's logbook. Pete had flown with our squadron, and was killed on March 31st. There had been no mission that day, and he and I were just stooging around Debden keeping in practice. I landed first; Pete flicked over on his back while making the last turn into the field, and plunged to the ground. It was a sad introduction to Pete's illustrious father.

That afternoon, the boys' parents arrived and their reunions with their sons were duly recorded by the ever-present newsreel cameramen. The two families dined together that evening at a Washington hotel. The following day they all returned to their hometowns. Johnny was greeted as a hero in Woonsocket by the mayor, who gave him the keys to the city. After an open-car parade, Johnny spoke to the crowd on Main Street. At home afterwards, he was delighted to find Lucky. The dog had been retrieved from the New York pet shop by Johnny's parents who had received a telegram from the thoughtful *Ile de France* steward.

There followed a whirl of activity interspersed with visits from friends and relatives. There was also an offer from a radio network in New York for Johnny and Don to appear on a radio show, for which they would each receive $500 and all expenses, including those of their parents if they wished to attend. They accepted and in New York were feted around the town.

Back in Woonsocket, Johnny was swamped with functions that he was required to attend – everything from war bond rallies, to men and women's clubs, to schools, to boy scout meetings. His classmates of 1940 at Woonsocket High School arranged a banquet for him and on and on it went through the entirety of his thirty-day leave. Of it all, only one event had meant much to him. He had been invited to attend a horse race named in his honour at the Pascoag Race Track and there he was introduced to a man named Jim Beattie and his two daughters, one of them, Joan, being the owner of a horse entered in the race. The name of the horse was Hidden Ace.

The story was much the same in Piqua, Ohio, when Don arrived there. The locals had begun a campaign to buy him a new Mustang to replace the one he had damaged. 'Ace Don Gentile Comes Home and All Piqua Goes Plain Nuts' read the headline in *The Stars and Stripes* a few weeks after Don had returned to his hometown. The date 25 May had been declared Don Gentile Day in Piqua, with a war bond rally and ceremonies honouring the returning hero and all those serving in the armed forces from Miami County, Ohio. The festivities began with a parade through downtown Piqua, with Don riding in the back of an open Ford convertible to Roosevelt Park, where tributes were paid to him and to three other veterans home from the war. He spoke briefly to the crowd, assuring them of his confidence in America's ability and determination to win the war. The following days saw Don, like Johnny, constantly pursued by eager newsmen both there in Ohio and on the personal appearance and bond rally tour that he and Johnny undertook.

During his leave, Don became reacquainted with a girl named Isabella Masdea, whom he had known when they were children. She lived in Columbus and they began dating and soon were engaged. Following the bond tour, Don was assigned to the Fighter Test Branch at Wright-Pattterson Air Force Base near Dayton as a test pilot.

In October, Don was elated to learn that his old friend and roommate at Debden, Steve Pisanos, was alive and well. Don had believed that Steve had been killed on the mission from which he had failed to return in early March. For six months after that mission, Steve had been evading the Germans in the Paris area while living and working with the French Resistance. After the Allies liberated Paris, Steve made his way back to England. He arrived at Debden on 2 September, when he learned that his old roommate and Johnny Godfrey were no longer there. Prohibited from flying combat missions again in the ETO, Steve returned to the States and was fortunate in also being assigned as a test pilot at Wright Field. There, he was reunited with Don and was happy to have the opportunity to fly a wide range of aircraft, including some of the captured German and Japanese fighter types.

Isabella and Don were married on 29 November 1944 with Steve as Don's best man. In July 1946, Don would return the favour as best man when Steve married Sophie Pappas in Kansas City.

In January 1945, Steve was selected to go to the Air Force Test Pilot School, which Don had already attended. Later Don and he were assigned to the test facility at Muroc in the southern California high desert to participate in the service testing of the Lockheed YP-80 Shooting Star jet fighter. The war in Europe was still raging and the Army Air Force was anxious to counter Germany's new Me 262 jet fighter with the Lockheed plane. But, with the end of the European war in May, the service test programme, which was near completion, was removed from 'expedited priority' status and Steve and Don were reassigned to Wright Field to work on other projects.

As their 30-day leave wore on, Johnny was actually looking forward to it ending. Playing the hero in the Air Force-orchestrated publicity operation was not to his liking, and it seemed that his time was never his own. He was relieved as the leave neared an end, to receive his orders requiring him to report to Hillsgrove Airfield near Providence, where he was to be an instructor. He still hoped to be able to return to Debden and the group at the earliest opportunity, however. Before beginning his duties at Hillsgrove, Johnny arranged to spend a few days visiting JJ and his wife, Virginia. Johnny was pleased at how well JJ's leg seemed to be healing and enjoyed reliving old times with his good friend. For the next two weeks, he was immersed in mundane flying duties by day, relieved in the evenings by time spent with his dad and friends playing cribbage in their local pub. The gunnery instruction experience did not go particularly well, as Johnny found that the target-shooting technique at Hillsgrove was not compatible with his own approach to shooting, honed as it had been in actual air combat. He was severely reprimanded for doing things his way rather than the local army way, and felt that he needed some help in the situation. He called in a favour from a colonel he knew at the Pentagon and the very next day received orders to return to England. This time, he decided, it would be wise to leave Lucky behind, and better for the dog. Sadly, Johnny would later learn that Lucky was run over and killed by a car after he had returned to England.

His first stop *en route* to the UK was the Ritz Carlton Hotel on the beach in Atlantic City, where he learned from his mother that the highly regarded news correspondent Lowell Thomas, had just been in touch with Don and wanted to write their story. It would mean considerable financial reward to them both, but would require them to remain in the US for an additional six months. Johnny wanted nothing more than to return to England as quickly as possible and a few days later he boarded the *Queen Elizabeth* for the transatlantic journey.

Only six of the sixty former RAF pilots that Johnny had arrived with at Debden just ten months earlier were still there. The Fourth Fighter Group no longer felt like home to him. His old crew chief, Larry Krantz, was still there, as was his friend and squadron mate Freddie Glover. Glover had been shot down over France three and a half months before and had evaded and escaped the Germans by walking over the Pyrenees mountains into Spain. Blakeslee was still running the group.

His time away from the Fourth Fighter Group had left Johnny rusty and in need of flying practice, as well as physical conditioning to withstand the effect of G forces in the turns of aerial combat. He worked at regaining his form for a week or so before deciding he was again combat ready. He celebrated his 'return' by beating up the field that early summer evening.

The next day he was on the list to fly the mission and he wondered if the long lay-off had affected his shooting ability.

His new wingman was Lieutenant Otey Glass. Twenty miles from Hamburg, they spotted a train and Johnny dived on it with Glass covering him. Johnny shot up the locomotive and Glass attacked the box cars. The pair then followed the rail line for about ninety miles to the south-west, finding and destroying seven more locomotives on the way. They then came across an airfield and Johnny told Glass to orbit just above the range of the ground fire while he strafed the seven Ju 52 transports sitting on the field. Destroying one of the planes, he went out and turned to make another run. Now the element of surprise was gone and the airfield defence guns were in action. By his third pass, he was receiving ground fire, yet he was so determined to build up his score that he came back for a fourth and then a fifth pass. The intensity of the flak now was such that he felt he had to break off the attack, but not before returning to get some gun camera images of the burning Ju 52s – two destroyed and three damaged. Then an Bf 109 appeared below them and Johnny went after it, firing the only two guns he had that were still operable. The German fighter exploded, capping a big day for Johnny.

CHAPTER TEN

Downed

Johnny Godfrey had returned to England, eager to resume combat flying with the group. However, shortly after arriving at Debden, he was embroiled in controversy. As their fame and exploits became widely known, both he and Gentile had been the subjects of many newspaper, magazine and radio interviews. Never shy in expressing his opinions, one of Johnny's quoted statements (from a conversation in the bar at Debden that he had believed to be off the record) had attracted the attention and aroused the ire of someone at the War Department in Washington. He received a cable asking if he was familiar with US Army Regulation six-hundred-and-something, governing the clearance of public statements made by serving army officers. Godfrey had struck a wrong note with the Department when the following item appeared in newspapers across America:

Captain John T. Godfrey, Rhode Island's leading fighter ace, is 'burned up' by what he calls America's present policy of 'spoon-feeding' its thousands of future combat pilots. 'I stood six days of their constant silly restrictions at Hillsgrove, RI, and then I said to hell with it and went back home' he told a United Press reporter. 'They won't let the kids fly when it's cloudy. They won't let them do this or that – until it makes you ill. They wouldn't let me fly the Ohio River with a 2,000-foot ceiling. I can remember taking off in England when you jumped straight into overcast and stayed that way up to 30,000 feet or more,' Godfrey added. He expressed the opinion that a kid-glove policy by 'brass hats' in this country is endangering the lives of all youngsters now in training camps . . . 'I figure it's a lot better to take risks and get better pilots,' he said. 'If the boys are spoon-fed at home it makes it mighty tough fitting them into combat outfits.'

It was only his status as one of the outstanding warriors of the USAAF that saved him from a court martial. Instead, he received a week's confinement to the base and a post-graduate course in proscriptive regulation. He was told to go and sin no more. By 5 August Johnny was back at work and, six hours later, as the Debden Mustangs were letting down over the field, he racked *Reggie's Reply* over in a spectacular series of snap rolls to let everyone below know that he had had a particularly good day. He had destroyed a Bf 109 in air combat, as well as three more Bf 109s and eight locomotives in ground strafing. On the ground, he let it be known that his goal was to score fifty enemy kills. No one at the base doubted either his determination or capability to achieve that goal. Most wondered, though, whether his luck would continue to hold.

Since D-Day, aerial encounters with German aircraft had been fewer and fewer, and the pilots of the Fourth Fighter Group were compelled to attack ground targets with ever increasing frequency. It was the most hazardous type of mission they flew – shooting at ground targets ranging from locomotives and railroad box cars, to flak towers, to aircraft on enemy airdromes.

Johnny was leading his four-plane section on 6 August near Berlin when he spotted a lone enemy aircraft well below their altitude. He called to his pilots: 'I'm going down at 3 o'clock to us. I see a Jerry at 2,000 feet.' Rolling over on his back, he dived on the unsuspecting Messerschmitt 410, his three section mates following him down in the bounce. Being careful to avoid the enemy rear gunner, he set up for a 30-degree deflection shot, aiming first for the tail and then tracking the fire along the fuselage. Johnny fired on the twin-engined fighter-bomber at very close range, causing flames to erupt from both engines. The enemy pilot jumped clear but his 'chute failed to open. Johnny followed the fiery Me 410 towards the earth, recording its demise on cine film.

The four Mustangs continued eastward beyond Berlin at 1,000 feet and then turned south-west. Freddie Glover saw two Bf 109s approaching an aerodrome far below and about to land. He reported the sighting to Johnny. Johnny's windscreen was partially covered in oil from the burning Me 410, obstructing his forward vision. He craned to sight on a Dornier Do-17 at the far end of the field. Firing on it, he saw the enemy aircraft explode as the Americans arrived over the aerodrome. Now the flak was intense and instantaneous and Johnny's P-51 was hit, but apparently not seriously. Freddie Glover flamed one of the Bf 109s. The Germans were on target and a machine-gun round shattered Johnny's windscreen. He recounted:

The windshield in front of the gunsight looked like a cobweb with a small hole in the centre. I felt a sharp tug on my left temple as the bullet creased me before it splat into the armour plate by my head. For a second the concussion of the bullet knocked me senseless, but I came to with my plane climbing. I could feel blood dripping down my forehead. Quickly I adjusted my goggles. They were close-fitting and I hoped they would keep the blood from running into my eyes. But I knew I was lucky. If it hadn't been for the oil on the windshield I would have been peering into the ring sight – and would have caught the bullet squarely between my eyes.

The other three Mustangs of his section caught up with him and he was shaken when Glover yelled on the R/T: 'Johnny, you're streaming glycol.' Checking his instruments, Johnny realised with horror that his engine temperature was already up in the red zone. The big Merlin would either seize or possibly blow up quite soon. He began to feel panic overwhelming him as he struggled to stay calm and think logically. He was still climbing and now tried to pull the emergency release to shed the canopy from its rails. He was shaking and had to use both hands in the effort. Then the canopy tore free, sending a mighty blast of frigid air through the cockpit. All he had to do at that point, he thought, was to undo his harness straps and step outside. A vision of the doomed German flier he had just witnessed falling with his malfunctioning parachute flashed through his mind. Trying to sound calm, he screamed: 'I'm baling out, boys. Tell Charlotte I'll see her when I get back.'

He had grabbed his leather helmet and earphones to pull them from his head in preparation to jump, when he heard the calm voice of Freddie Glover. His friend said: 'Don't jump, Johnny, there's still a chance. Now sit back and relax for a second. You're still flying and the plane won't blow up. Look at your instruments and tell me how your oil pressure is.' The reading was normal and Glover told Johnny to unscrew the wobble pump and start priming the engine to force raw gas into the cylinders, creating the same effect as the glycol. He said he had heard of someone else doing that and it worked. The wobble pump was on the instrument panel and had a small handle like the starting handle on an outboard motor. When pulled, it would spring back into position. Using his right hand, Johnny pulled out the pump handle and released it again to feed the gas into the cylinders. He continued the action, though the pump did not operate easily.

'It's working, Freddie. My engine temperature is moving away from the danger zone.'

'Good, Johnny. Now throttle back and don't push your engine. Try to keep climbing. The higher we go the cooler the air will be – every little bit helps.'

Throttling back, Johnny began a slow climb, while continuing to work the wobble pump. When they reached 18,000 feet, Glover and his wingman departed. He had done all he could to help and now the task of pumping and bringing the Mustang back to Debden was left entirely to Johnny. Johnny's wingman, a pilot named Patteau, stuck with him, protecting his tail from attack. When hit, his aircraft had been 675 miles from Debden and now he worked the pump as hard as he could to keep his engine going.

He calculated that he was working the pump sixteen times a minute and would have to continue to do so for another three hours, or nearly 3,000 gas injections, if he was to make it back to base. But the bitter, biting cold air blasting through the cockpit was so painful that he doubted if he could survive that much more exposure, even if his aeroplane did. Then, his engine sputtered and quit. He quickly flipped the switch to the reserve tank position. The engine started again and, checking his instruments, Johnny found that he had less than forty gallons of fuel remaining. He realised, too, that he did not know his exact position.

Unable to stand the intense cold any longer, Johnny began to descend and saw the Channel coast up ahead. The Mustang dropped gently through the 4,000-foot cloud level as he crossed the coast of Holland. The flying glove on his right hand had worn through at the palm from the friction of working the wobble pump and his blisters had now become slippery, bleeding flesh, causing the pump handle to slip from his grasp. The wind blast, though somewhat warmer at the lower altitude, was still tornado-like and he now had serious doubts that he could continue pumping much longer. That, and the tiny amount of fuel remaining, caused him to call to his wingman: 'Patty, I don't think I have enough gas to make it. Call Air Sea Rescue for a fix. I'm switching over now.' He hit the button to set his radio on the Rescue frequency and listened as his wingman made the call and received a heading to the nearest airfield, Beccles. It was twenty-one minutes' flying time to the airfield. Now, at least, if he did have to bale out, he felt confident that a seaplane would be sent out to pick him up within minutes. The questions were, did he have enough gas to make it to Beccles, and could he somehow keep working that damned plunger long enough to reach safety?

He could and he did. He arrived at Beccles, exhausted. He didn't bother with niceties like circling the field, wind direction or other air traffic. He simply put the Mustang down as best he could and rolled out to a point on the grass. He climbed out of the aircraft and lit a cigarette.

That night Johnny shoved a five-pound note on the bar in front of Freddie Glover. 'I want to see how drunk you can get, Freddie – and if that runs out, come a-running. I owe you quite a few for today.'

Grover Hall recounted the fateful mission flown by Johnny on 24 August:

Lt Melvin N. Dickey, of Tampa, Fla. set three Ju 52s on fire on his first pass over the drome [eight miles north-west of Nordhausen, Germany]. The flak was coming up through the black smoke plumes as the Mustangs zigzagged in. Holding the throttle to the firewall and fish-tailing his craft to disconcert the ground gunners, Godfrey held his forehead to the gunsight and blazed away, destroying four Jus to bring his score to 36, the most enemy planes an American pilot had destroyed to date.

He was rocked about in the cockpit and his craft wobbled as a burst of flak riddled it. Godfrey shrank from looking at his instruments as he guessed the engine was catching fire.

'Oh, what the hell?' he said to himself. That was a memorable feature of Godfrey's combat personality. He could get rattled and frightened to the point of panic, and at the same time shed it and demonstrate a remarkable degree of reckless, careless aggressiveness. He had returned from the States exhausted by the activity attendant upon bond rallies and night-clubbing. He had flown every mission since returning; he was oppressed and worn by the repeated sight of his friends being maimed and drowned. His six feet two inches were gaunt, his long fingers had a tremble, his eyes were tired, but he kept spearing himself back into the muzzle of the German guns. Combat was a tar baby he couldn't let go of. He was so exhausted, as sometimes happened to pilots, that on occasion he wanted to cry. Getting shot down would virtually be a relief, a way to escape the crazy pattern of living that ensnared him.

So to hell with whatever might be wrong with his plane. He made three more attacks on the burning drome as the group criss-crossed the field. Godfrey saw the smoke billowing back from his plane. Pumping the primer wouldn't keep it alive this time. He had been operating on borrowed time. This was the default.

'Johnny here,' they heard him say. 'This is it . . . tell Charlotte . . .' The plane stalled out a bare 30 feet above the ground and as it bellied into a meadow, his forehead banged against the gunsight, knocking him out. He groped for his consciousness, instinctively fearing he would be burned in the plane.

I've got to get out, Johnny thought. He worked to undo his harness. His hand trembled and for a time he couldn't pull the canopy back to escape. He struggled to climb from the cockpit, but was held fast by his parachute pack until he remembered to turn the quick-release. Free of the aircraft, he started to run, before realising that he had forgotten his escape kit and had not pressed the button that would blow up the IFF (Identification Friend or Foe) device in the Mustang. He went back for the kit and the first aid package, pausing just long enough to hit the IFF detonator button. When he reached the other end of the ploughed field where he had crash-landed, he looked back at his aircraft, which was nearly consumed by flames. At that moment, Mel Dickey buzzed Johnny in a farewell salute. Then it was eerily quiet. He had never felt more alone.

Johnny staggered to a nearby wood and blacked-out again. He took Benzedrine tablets and ran most of the day, desperate to get as far away from his aircraft as he could. He quenched an extreme thirst by sinking his feet in mudholes to squeeze out the water. Hours later, he stopped to rest in a wood and was finally aware of the pain and the blood from the open wound on the side of his head. He opened the escape kit. It contained a map, money, a small compass, some cigarettes, matches and chocolate. Lighting one of the cigarettes, he opened the map of Germany and tried to determine his present location. Remembering his approximate position prior to the crash-landing, he was able to estimate his present position as roughly 130 miles from the French border. He gathered his meagre provisions and began walking again.

By early evening he came to a little stream and decided to spend the night there. He was suffering from painful blisters on his feet as well as from the pain of his head wound. He injected himself with a morphine syrette from his escape kit and lay down to rest or die – he didn't much care which.

At 4 am he awoke. His head felt clearer and he lay in the heart of Germany, looking at his watch and thinking. The boys would have been briefed and they would be just about crossing over the Channel now. All through the day he would look at his watch to mark the events at Debden: they're in the bar now . . . everybody buying beer because it's the end of the month . . . they're walking down by the Aero Club to the cinema . . . He lay concealed beside a railroad track, planning to hide in the coal tender of a France-bound train. However, a trail of blood led a German farmer to him.

On the way to Dulag-Luft, the German interrogation camp near Frankfurt, where many Allied airmen spent their early days of captivity, Captain Johnny Godfrey was led through a small town. The angry residents threw stones and spat at him.

His tiny cell at the interrogation centre was furnished with a cot and straw-filled mattress, which took up three-quarters of the space. There was a small barred window at the end. He was left in isolation for five days and nights. Then, a cheery visitor arrived, all smiles and apologies for the circumstances in which the pilot found himself. 'I, sir, am the official representative of the American Red Cross,' he stated, offering Johnny a cigarette and light. 'Now, in order to let your folks know that you are safe, I have here a Red Cross form for you to fill out.' Johnny took the form and read the information required: name, rank, serial number, age, home town, parents' names, unit attached to before being shot down, type of aircraft . . . 'Under the laws of the Geneva Convention I am obliged to give only my name, rank and serial number. If you wish, I will gladly furnish them,' he said. The smile disappeared as the 'Red Cross' man snatched the form and the cigarette from the pilot and left the room in a fury.

Later that day Johnny was led down the corridor and into another building, where he was welcomed by an American-sounding voice in a *Luftwaffe* uniform. 'Captain Godfrey, welcome to Dulag-Luft, my name is Hans. I trust you will not mind if I call you John. Cigarette?'

He stood facing the interrogator, who asked him about the attacks that the American pilots were making on the German aerodromes. Johnny responded, as he had been trained to do, with his name, rank and serial number. The interrogator tried to shock and confuse him by mentioning several Fourth Fighter Group pilots and several facts about them that virtually no one outside of Debden could know. If the remarks surprised Johnny, he didn't show it. During the conversation he learned that Hans had been born in Germany, but had lived for twenty years in New York. The interrogator was about thirty-five years old, intelligent and quite witty.

Following the interview, Johnny was taken to a new cell, much larger than the first and with two windows. In it was a small bureau on which lay a towel, soap and shaving equipment. He was then taken to a washroom where he was allowed to shower and shave. Back in his room he began to think about escaping again. He vowed not to repeat the mistakes he had made in the days after he was shot down. His next escape attempt would be well-planned. He would move only by night, carry ample food and drinking water and would do all he could in preparation for the attempt, to get himself in shape for the effort. He would practise walking as much as possible to strengthen his leg muscles.

The next day, Johnny received a note from Hans: 'The officers of Dulag-Luft wish to invite you as guest of honour for dinner at 7 o'clock. Formal dress not required.' Just before 7 pm, a guard came to escort him from the compound, through an attractive formal garden and into an adjoining officers' mess. In the centre of the room was a large table with eight men seated around it. On the table lay a huge assortment of salads, cheeses, cold cuts and other food. Most of the guests were speaking English fluently. When Johnny was seated with them, an orderly appeared with a glass for the American. Champagne was poured and the guests toasted 'The Führer'. Under his breath, Johnny drank to the US. In a few moments, another guest entered the room and introduced himself as 'Gabby Gabreski'. He wore the silver leaf of a USAAF lieutenant-colonel. Johnny thought the man might be an impostor, but changed his mind after asking Gabreski several pointed questions. Gabreski had been shot down a month before and was one of the great aces of the Eighth Air Force's 56th Fighter Group. Sharing the brief time with him did wonders for Johnny's morale.

The next afternoon he was taken to an adjoining building, where thirty other American airmen were awaiting transportation to a permanent prisoner-of-war camp. Each was given a Red Cross food parcel containing candy, cigarettes, canned milk, canned meat, sugar, soap, a razor and Nescafé. For two days and three nights they travelled by train across Germany to Sagan in Silesia, Stalag-Luft III. At the Sagan camp, the Americans were strip-searched. They dressed again, were each given a metal plate with their name, rank and PoW number on it, and were photographed. The camp was surrounded by a wire fence twenty feet high. There were guard towers at the corners with four manned machine-guns in each. Rolls of barbed wire were scattered randomly along the base of the fence. A single strand of wire four feet above the ground completely encircled the enclosure about twenty feet inside the fence. The guards had orders to shoot anyone who stepped between the wire and the fence.

In the stalags run by the *Luftwaffe*, captured airmen found themselves in a new kind of war . . . one of grinding boredom and monotony. The prisoners were known as *kriegies*, from the German word *krieg*, for war. In the morning of his first full day at Sagan, Johnny was given his clothing issue, consisting of two shirts, one pair of trousers, one woollen hat, a dozen handkerchiefs, six pairs of socks, a heavy overcoat, two towels and two changes of bed linen. He soon encountered other downed pilots from the Fourth Fighter Group: Waterman, Millikan, Edner, McDill and Wynn. They were all anxious to have news of Debden and the group.

As he settled in to *kriegie* life, Johnny surveyed his environment, collecting information that would be useful when an escape opportunity presented itself. He noted that the half-mile long, quarter-mile wide rectangle that was his compound had recently been a part of the forest; the trees had been cut down but the stumps remained throughout the area. Within the compound were twenty-four barracks laid out four abreast and six deep. There were eight rooms in each barracks, a lavatory and a small room with a cook stove. Each barracks was erected on log pilings two feet above the ground so that the guards, known as ferrets, could crawl underneath to look for any tunnelling activity. Each room contained twelve bunks. Every man had been given a knife and fork. No plates, pans or utensils had been issued and the prisoners had to make them by hand from Red Cross parcel ration cans. The Germans provided only meagre rations and the food had little nutritional value. The men depended heavily on the Red Cross food parcels.

Every day – at eight in the morning and four in the afternoon – the residents of each barracks lined up on the parade ground area of the compound while German guards conducted an *appel* or count, to be certain that none of the *kriegies* had escaped. No one was allowed out of his barracks between eight at night and seven the next morning. Lights-out was at 10 pm After that, the entire area was patrolled by guards with Alsatian police dogs.

While his mind focused almost entirely on escaping, Johnny knew that the odds were stacked against him. In 1943 a large group of RAF officers had tunnelled their way to freedom in what has since been called 'The Great Escape'. Most of the men were recaptured and, on orders from Hitler, fifty were executed; they were shot in the back of the head. In those days, a formalised escape committee had operated to assist and advise any prisoners who were planning escape attempts. Following the 1943 mass escape, the committee ceased to function. After an early effort to cut through the barbed wire and the fence beyond, Johnny and a few other *kriegies* were thwarted when the heavy-duty pliers they had procured proved insufficient to the task.

Winter came and both the prisoners and the Germans began to realise that the end was near for the Third Reich, as sporadic reports of Allied advances in German territory circulated. On 28 January, the prisoners of Stalag-Luft III were informed that they were to be marched from the camp that night, to another location. It was the coldest winter in decades, with two feet of snow on the ground and the temperature averaging below zero. When the march began, it was snowing heavily. Most of the men wore their entire clothing issue, but as they walked many became overheated and had to discard some of their clothing. Many tried to bring all of their possessions: extra shoes, blankets, pots and pans, food and miscellaneous equipment. As they struggled in the blowing snow to keep up with the column, most had to lighten their load and much of what they had brought lay strewn in their wake. Johnny thought that the trudging column of prisoners looked like 'animals being herded to market'.

The men were allowed to stop and rest for five minutes each hour. Owing to the reduced nutrition of their diet, most of the marchers were unfit for such exertion and were nearly exhausted by noon on the first day. They had to continue until 5 pm, however, before shelter could be found for them in the barns of a small village. There, they were able to boil water for instant coffee and help themselves to milk from a cow in their sleeping quarters. Exhaustion was universal that night. Everyone slept soundly and no one had the energy to attempt escape.

The next afternoon, in near darkness, Johhny noticed a couple of men sneak out of the column and disappear between two buildings in the small village they had entered. He decided instantly to try to make a break too. He dodged away from the column and headed for the woods adjoining the village. Now the snow was swirling and up to four feet deep. He had no compass and no stars to guide him. He rested frequently, but felt the cold gradually numbing his entire body. Dog-tired, he became thoroughly discouraged, believing that he had just been walking in circles. He lay down under the shelter of some branches, wrapped himself in his blanket and went to sleep. In the morning he woke, unable to feel his feet. Removing his boots and socks, he rubbed one foot and then the other. He realised that losing his feet to frostbite was too high a price to pay for freedom.

When he was able to walk again, he set off to locate the tracks of the marchers and rejoin them. When he reached the village of the previous evening, he came to a tavern and went in. There, an elderly German guard and four PoWs were sprawled in sleep. He woke them up, explained that he thought his feet were frozen and asked for help. Within fifteen minutes the prisoners had managed to produce some feeling in his feet by massaging them with snow. As his circulation slowly returned, the pain was excruciating. He learned that the four soldiers had all been wounded and unable to keep up with the other marchers. The guard had taken them to rest in the tavern and seemed in no rush to resume the march himself. He showed no interest in Johnny's experience, but agreed that he might be able to arrange a ride for them all if he could trade some of their cigarettes, coffee and sugar. The deal was struck and the guard departed after they pledged not to escape while he was gone. Before leaving, the guard laboriously wrote down the names and serial numbers of his five charges.

Thirty minutes later the guard was back, loaded down with six pounds of horse meat, two loaves of bread, eighteen potatoes, four swedes, two bunches of carrots and a half pound of fresh butter. The little group spent the rest of the day preparing 'the best stew any of them had ever eaten'. That night, for the first time in five months, they all slept with full stomachs. The next day a sleigh complete with bells arrived to transport them several miles to where they caught up with the marchers who were resting in a large pottery factory. It was stifling inside the building as the furnaces had been maintained at maximum heat for proper drying. A day later, the prisoners were on the road again, heading for Spremberg, which they reached at 2 am. There, a train of thirty boxcars awaited them. Neat stacks of Red Cross food parcel boxes were piled near each boxcar and forty men with a total of twenty Red Cross parcels were soon crammed into each of the freight cars. Sleeping had to be done in shifts, as all of the men could not lie down at the same time in the cramped space. The destination was Nuremberg.

As the long train crawled through the night, Johnny and other airmen, who themselves had often attacked and shot up German trains in the course of their missions, wondered whether other trigger-happy Allied fighter pilots would discover this train when daylight came.

At the Nuremberg camp, cooking and sanitation facilities were non-existent. The *kriegies* slept on bedding of old straw infested with vermin, which quickly re-located to the men. Nuremberg itself was a prime military target for the RAF, which had often visited the town by night. Many USAAF bombs had also fallen on the town. The *kriegies* could only hope that the pilots of the American and British fighters that regularly overflew the area had been briefed that it was a prisoner-of-war camp and not an army installation.

By March, the Red Cross food parcel shipments were diminishing. But the war news was positive and the *kriegies* were upbeat, believing that their chances of surviving the war were greatly improved, provided they didn't starve in the meantime. Air raid sirens sounded almost daily in the Nuremberg area and Allied bombers and fighters appeared more frequently as the winter yielded to spring. The prisoners clung to the hope that very soon Allied forces would liberate Germany and the PoW camps. Then, on 3 April, the camp officials ordered that the prisoners be marched to Munich the next day. Johnny Godfrey considered the order and decided to hell with it. He had done all the marching he could tolerate and he believed that, as the American forces approached, the Germans might well decide to kill all the prisoners. He had located a manhole cover between two of the camp compounds and that evening he enlisted the help of an officer, who agreed to provide some extra food and water for Johnny's next escape attempt. That night, the officer helped him remove the manhole cover and hide with his provisions in the space below, before replacing the cover. Later, Johnny heard lengthy machine-gun firing. He spent all the next day in the manhole, listening, until he was certain that everyone had departed.

That night the RAF bombed Nuremberg again, leaving Johnny temporarily deaf in his hidey hole. The next day, claustrophobia and the stale air of the hole drove him to risk raising the manhole cover. The area appeared to be deserted and was deathly quiet. He spent that night in the hole. In the morning it began to rain, lightly at first and then torrentially. The water was pouring into the manhole and soon he elected to leave. It was darkening as he emerged. There was no sign of life. He was suddenly buoyed by a feeling of release. He had ample food, fresh water and a blanket, and was convinced that this time he would make it.

All he had to do was head west. He walked through fields and woods until the first light of dawn, when he found cover in a wood. He slept through the day until dusk, when he woke refreshed and famished. He dined on a can of bully beef and resumed his journey. Hours later he came upon a house and barn.

With Allied forces nearing the area, the farmer, and his daughter, proved exceedingly helpful when the American pilot identified himself. They fed him, provided a bath and a place to sleep, as well as some old work clothes to wear in place of his army uniform and some food to carry with him. The farmer also alerted Johnny to the presence of some German SS troops in the area, helping him to avoid them. In return, Johnny wrote a note, which he left with the farmer. It read: 'To any American; Please extend all courtesies possible and help to the bearer of this note. He helped me while escaping.' (After the war, Godfrey was able to obtain the farmer's name and address with the help of an army chaplain. For two years he sent food parcels to the farmer.)

His energy and spirits renewed and his pack reprovisioned, Johnny Godfrey again struck out for freedom, walking with the North Star over his right shoulder as a guide. The next day, he encountered two American PoWs, Sergeants Joe Silverman and Ray Donahue. They had been in the Sergeants' Compound near him at Nuremberg and had escaped during the machine-gunning that he had heard. Johnny recalled:

I explained how I had hid in the camp and heard the firing. 'That's when we escaped,' said Silverman. 'The guards weren't firing at us; they were firing at two P-47s that had flown the length of the column. When the guns opened up, everybody sprawled in the ditches. We just kept running, that's all.'

They walked in tandem through the woods and fields during the night, trying to keep parallel with the road. Meeting no one, they assumed that they had not been noticed. Stopping just twice to rest, they huddled together in their blankets for extra warmth. With the dawn, they began looking for a hiding place to spend the day.

Carefully skirting an open field, they entered woods on the other side, when they heard, 'Halt!' A member of the German home army approached them through the trees. Instinctively, the three men began to run. The first of three shots were fired in their direction. One slammed into a tree near Johnny, the other two scattering leaves in their path. The three halted instantly, putting their arms up. They all realised that the German was deadly serious, his Luger pistol pointing threateningly at Johnny's chest. The German also seemed nervous and they all sensed that it was imperative not to provoke him. Other soldiers now approached and the three were soon being searched for weapons. Then they were told to follow the German who had captured them. As they walked through the woods, they noticed foxholes on both sides of them. They had stumbled into a German stronghold.

Three German officers were studying maps in the clearing ahead. They dropped the maps and looked questioningly at the American trio. One of the Germans, who spoke a little English, asked them what they were doing. Johnny explained that they had been *en route* from one prison camp to the other when an American aircraft had strafed them; they had run into the woods but couldn't find their way back. When the German officer asked them which camp, John informed him that it was Nuremberg. He smirked and said, 'You are lost all right, Nuremberg is seventy-five kilometres away from here.' The officer had been watching Joe while he was talking, and asked him what his name was. 'Sergeant Joe Silverman, sir.' The officer's face contorted in anger. 'Jew bastard,' he said and spat in Joe's face. Johnny was dumbfounded, then furious. The tension was broken by the arrival of P-47s.

With the roar of the Thunderbolt engines, the German officer began barking orders. He ordered the Americans to sit with their backs to a small tree in the centre of the clearing and told them that he had ordered his troops to shoot them if they moved. There was one small tree in the middle of the clearing. Then the P-47s commenced the first of many strafing passes, peppering the woods with machine-gun fire. Broken branches fell around the three men, who heard cries of pain in the lulls between firing. The noise of gunfire was deafening. A brief lull ensued when the ammunition of the aircraft was, apparently, exhausted. Soon though, more aircraft appeared – dive-bombers this time. The Americans were pressed heavily against the tree by the concussions of the bombs.

They were also being pelted by shards of wood, dirt clods, bits of German equipment and human flesh. They choked on the dust and smoke. All around them lay broken trees and wounded men. Then the aircraft left and calm enveloped the wood.

The three Americans were unhurt. Order slowly returned. The uninjured Germans crawled from their dugouts and lit cigarettes. One offered cigarettes to the Americans, who took them gratefully and anxiously awaited their fate. In the late afternoon the German officer returned and ordered the Americans to stand. 'You three are going back where you came from – and consider yourselves lucky I didn't have you shot for spies.' He wrote a note and gave it to one of his soldiers, and the Americans were marched off.

When they came out of the woods, they saw what the dive-bombers had been after – the smoking remains of a troop train, whose coaches had been ripped apart and tossed on their sides against the embankments. Sections of track were uprooted from the ties and twisted from the force of the explosions. Soldiers worked at salvaging equipment.

As they walked eastward along the road towards Nuremberg, their guard tried unsuccessfully to obtain transportation for them. During the day, there was no traffic on the road; trucks were parked, not daring to move, afraid of the American raids. The boys saw Mustangs, Thunderbolts, Spitfires and Typhoons flying low over the road, in search of military targets. At night, the road was in chaos with trucks coming and going and road blocks set up to try to stem the tide of civilians fleeing the advancing Americans troops.

Shortly before midnight on 13 April, they stopped in a small village and the guard was able to obtain a ride for them back to Nuremberg. The old truck drove slowly and was carrying about twenty people in the back. It stopped at the outskirts of Nuremberg and all the passengers got down from the back. Somehow, the guard found his way through the rubble caused by the raids by the RAF and USAAF. They reached the north gates of the prison camp at 7 am, and stood a quarter of a mile from where Johnny had escaped nine days earlier. No one bothered to register them. Again, they were behind barbed wire.

Hearing the whine of more shells, the boys wondered if the Americans knew this was a PoW camp. If not, it was likely that more PoWs would be killed. An US Army lieutenant with them wanted to try and reach the American lines to inform them and Johnny told him he would go along with him if they could somehow get out of the compound.

The two men ran along the edge of the outside fence to the gate. There, they explained to the German guard what they wanted to do and he handed them his rifle, but not wishing to be caught with the weapon, they refused it. They opened the gate and ran down the length of the now empty compound until they reached the road. There, advancing in single file on both sides of the road, were American GIs. Shouting happily and waving their arms, the pair ran towards the American column and asked the GIs if they knew the PoW camp was nearby. They said that some other PoWs had brought them the news earlier that morning. Apparently, it had been German 88 mm guns that had been firing on them earlier. The lieutenant in charge of the platoon told Johnny that they were heading for the camp to take charge of the PoWs in it.

Johnny asked if that included himself and his companion. 'All my orders say is to take charge of the PoWs in the camp. If you boys are lucky you can make Paris tonight. The Americans have a landing strip forty miles south-west of here, which they are using to bring in supplies. Everything is secure in back of us, so best of luck.'

The officer then marched off with his platoon. Johnny and his lieutenant friend headed in the opposite direction, anxious to get as far away as possible from the PoW camp. They soon passed a ditch in which two dead German soldiers lay grotesquely on their sides. In one of the German's hands was a Belgian .32 automatic pistol. Johnny grabbed it as his only souvenir of the war.

They soon encountered several American jeeps and trucks. A passing jeep stopped and the driver enquired where the two men were heading. Johnny responded, 'To the nearest field kitchen.' 'Hop in,' said the sergeant, 'and I'll drop you off by one.'

Five miles down the road, the sergeant stopped the jeep in front of a building, fragrant with the aroma of baking bread. Incredibly, the staff sergeant in charge of the kitchen was from Woonsocket, Johnny's home-town; not only that, he had worked for Johnny's father at the American Wringer Company. 'Not content with giving us food, he brought two bottles of champagne, so we drank champagne, instead of coffee, for breakfast.'

CHAPTER ELEVEN

Two-man Air Force

As the train approached Audley End that spring day in 1945, Johnny was moved by the verdant beauty of the English countryside. It had been eight months since he had last seen it – eight months he had spent as a prisoner of the Germans. At Debden, the base hadn't changed much in the time he had been away, but nearly all the faces were unfamiliar. He knew almost no one and didn't pause to reminisce or reflect. He went directly to see the Intelligence Officer to discuss his claims of enemy aircraft destroyed on his final mission. Lacking his combat film of the mission, he had only his word about the claims. The officer arranged for them to view gun camera film of his wingman for that day. At one point in the screening, Johnny was startled when he saw his own aircraft enter the frame, while his wingman was firing at one of the Ju 52s on the airfield ahead of them. He knew then that, instead of waiting until he had finished his pass, the wingman had commenced firing before Johnny could get out of the way. He had been shot down by the man who was supposedly protecting him. He considered the irony of the incident. The wingman had been awarded a Distinguished Flying Cross for the mission; the 'wingman principle' that had brought Johnny fame had ultimately brought him down and led to his becoming a prisoner-of-war. His claims for the mission were never confirmed.

Johnny was in London on VE Day. He watched the hundreds of thousands of civilian and military revellers dancing in the streets, finally able to celebrate the end of the war in Europe. With mixed emotions, he resolved to forget Debden and think only of the future. He used the time onboard ship returning to America to eat heartily, in an effort to regain some of the weight he had lost as a PoW.

There was no hero's welcome awaiting him in Rhode Island this time. Nor did he expect one. He realised that Americans, like people every-where, were sick and tired of the war and he looked forward to a relatively quiet thirty-day leave, much of it at home with his family. The USAAF had given him $2,000 in back pay and he planned to buy a car with part of the money.

Late in May, Johnny was again invited to the races, this time to Narragansett Race Track, where he was asked to present a cup to the winner of the feature race of the day. Once again, he encountered Jim Beattie, who was accompanied by his daughter Joan. This time Johnny paid more attention to the young girl and from then on their relationship grew.

Jim Beattie had earned his fortune in the lace-making business. He had been born in Long Eaton, England, the centre of the lace trade, and had worked for eighteen years in a lace mill. With his small savings, his wife and a four-month-old daughter, he had sailed for the United States, where he had struggled to save enough money to buy his first lace-making machine, which he set up in a barn in Coventry, Rhode Island. The business grew through the 1930s and he prospered. Sadly, in 1938 his wife died. During the war, the lace business grew and Jim became the largest racehorse owner in the state.

In August 1945, Johnny was still in the USAAF and received orders to report to Craig Field, Alabama. He asked Joan to be his wife and they were married by a justice of the peace in Selma, Alabama, on 23 August. Newspapers across America carried the story, 'Air Force Hero Marries Socialite'.

Johnny had brief stints in the Air Force fighter test programme at Wright Field, Dayton, Ohio, where he was reunited with both Don Gentile and Steve Pisanos, and then with Don at the Globe Aircraft Company in Fort Worth, Texas. Johnny then acceded to Joan's pleas to give up flying for a chance to learn the lace business in his father-in-law's company.

His relationship with his boss/father-in-law was frequently stormy, but he worked hard at learning the business. Eventually, with the help and encouragement of Beattie, he was able to start his own lace-making operation, which was soon growing dramatically. With 110 people on his payroll and thirty-five machines generating substantial profit on the floors of his mill, he suddenly found that he had very little to do. When Jim's foreman at the Linwood plant quit, Johnny offered to do that job in addition to running his own mill at night. His responsibilities increased greatly, but still he sought new challenges.

In 1952 Johnny was asked by the Republican town committee of West Greenwich, Rhode Island, to run for the state senate. It was a good year for the Republicans. Dwight Eisenhower was elected to the US presidency and Johnny Godfrey to the Rhode Island senate. In 1954, Johnny was asked by the officials of his party to consider running for Governor of the state. He did – consider it – but decided against it. By July of that year, the first signs of the disease that would ultimately kill him appeared. After due deliberation, he resigned from the various positions he held in the lace industry to try and find some contentment in what remained of his life. Johnny, Joan and their children moved to the seaside town of South Freeport, Maine, in August.

Amyotrophic Lateral Sclerosis is an insidious, incurable disease of the nervous system. In the bright, sunny morning of 2 October 1956, Johnny was told by his doctor that he had ALS and could look forward to a life expectancy of from six months to perhaps two years. Johnny was shocked. He and Joan held each other and cried uncontrollably. Then they determined to find a doctor who might offer them some hope. Johnny showed the same tenacity in his search for a cure, or at least some way of combating the most frightening enemy he had ever faced, that he had shown against enemy pilots during the Second World War. Ultimately, his quest took him to Germany, where Artur Boss, a Russian-born doctor, operated a clinic for the treatment of sclerosis diseases at Schwenningen. Johnny had learned that Dr Boss could offer him a slim chance, claiming to have successfully treated twenty-three of seventy-two cases. Naturally, the doctor could not guarantee success, and Johnny would need to come to Germany for the treatment, which would take one year. But in the belief that he had a one-in-three possibility of his disease being arrested, he made the trip.

To the limits of his strength and capability, he spent as much time as he could with his wife and two sons, sailing, fishing and hunting, which they all loved. The boys were named Bob and Jay after Johnny's close friends in the wartime USAAF.

The efforts to treat his illness produced only limited results that did not last. Johnny Godfrey lost his battle with the terrible wasting disease and died on 12 June 1958. He was 37.

In December 1947, during his time with Johnny at Globe Aircraft Company, where they were both Sales and Services Division Directors, Don Gentile was offered a regular Air Force commission. He was delighted to return to the service, where he would again be able to fly fighters. His initial assignment was to Tyndall AFB, Florida, where he attended the Air Tactical School. Then, in April 1949, he was assigned to US Air Force headquarters in Washington DC. In June, he enrolled in a two-year course at the University of Maryland, College Park, where he majored in Military Science under the Air University programme.

Early in January 1951, Don, his wife and their three sons, Don Jr, Joseph and Patrick, were preparing to move to Selfridge AFB, Michigan, where he had been reassigned. After attending Mass early on Sunday 28 January, he stayed at home with the children while Isabella went to church. He had decided to go for one more proficiency hop that afternoon in the T-33 jet trainer that he had been flying in recent weeks, before their move from Maryland to Michigan the next day. He would be accompanied on the flight by Sergeant Gregory D. Kirsch, whom he had previously promised a ride. The sergeant took the tandem back seat. After receiving clearance, Don applied take-off power and at 3.05 pm the jet lifted off the Andrews AFB runway. At 3.10 pm he descended and buzzed his apartment on Rowalt Drive in College Park to let Isabella know that he would be home soon. The Andrews tower operators observed Don's T-33 shortly thereafter at an altitude of 2,500 feet. He called the tower for a radio check and was told that they were reading him loud and clear. Don then began a descent and almost immediately the aircraft became uncontrollable. It began to level out and then to roll. Controllers in the Andrews tower then heard Don yelling to Sergeant Kirsch to eject. The sergeant, evidently frozen in fear or incapable of reacting in the situation, did not respond. At 3.18 pm a controller in Andrews tower sighted a large smoke cloud north-east of the base and notified Base Operations and the Crash Crew. The pilot of a Navy plane in the vicinity was requested to fly over the area to check it out. He quickly responded and reported to the tower that the smoke appeared to emanate from an aircraft crash. By 3.40 pm the base crash equipment had reached the scene of the crash near Forestville. The Crash Crew confirmed that the aircraft was that of Don and that the impact had occurred four and a half miles north-east of Andrews. Don and his passenger had been killed instantly.

Steve Pisanos, Don's old friend, roommate and best man, escorted Don's coffin on the overnight train journey from Maryland to Columbus, Ohio, for the funeral. The Chief of Staff of the USAF, General Hoyt S. Vandenberg, sent a telegram to Don's widow:

On behalf of the men and women of the United States Air Force, I extend deepest sympathy to you and your family on the untimely death of your husband, Major Don Gentile [he was promoted posthumously to Major]. As one of World War II's most noted aces, Major Gentile made an outstanding combat record. His loss will be keenly felt, not only by those who knew him personally, but throughout a country that knew him as a courageous fighter for freedom.

Having served as one of the pall bearers at Don's funeral, Steve Pisanos reflected more than half a century later: 'The loss of my closest wartime friend was a deep trauma, which I still feel in my heart to this day.'

Several years earlier, in January 1945, Lieutenant-General James H. Doolittle, Commander, Eighth Air Force, reported to the officers and enlisted personnel of the Eighth Air Force on its progress in the war to that point:

The year 1944 was a significant one for those who have devoted themselves to the cause of freedom and justice throughout the world. In both hemispheres, the forces of tyranny were rolled back and steadily compressed into surrounded bastions from which there can be no escape. Here in the European theatre, the Eighth Air Force fought with distinction. It contributed importantly to the Allied war effort and earned a place in history which time will not erase. As the Commander of the Force, I am responsible not only to my military superiors, but to those who have made the year so memorable – the men and women of the Eighth.

On December 24, 1944, the Eighth Air Force sent over Germany 2,034 heavy bombers and 936 fighters, the greatest single force of airplanes ever dispatched in history. Well over 21,000 Americans flew in that armada over marshalling yards, vital communications centres and airfields behind the enemy lines. Many times that number worked on the ground to launch those planes, and many more again per-formed the great varieties of services, which have built the Eighth into the deadly weapon it was intended to be.

The past year has seen the Eighth Air Force in full stride. We have hit the enemy with more than 430,000 tons of bombs. During the year, our fliers flew 1,700,000 operational hours, and our planes consumed 522,000,000 gallons of gasoline to release those tons of destruction. Blows were directed in turn at the types of targets which were most vital to the Nazi war effort and which could only be destroyed by precision bombing – the job of the Eighth.

Our first task was to make sure that when the combined Allied ground forces invaded 'Fortress Europe', we would have superiority in the air. Our bombers and fighters, hand in hand with those of the RAF, and the Ninth, Twelfth and Fifteenth American Air Forces, pounded German air power in the early months of the year, and the *Luftwaffe* was virtually helpless during the initial phases of the invasion. Aircraft factories, oil plants and supplies, and transportation facilities – these targets showed the effects of our pre-invasion hammering when D-Day came.

Our second great mission was performed during the invasion phase. Although designed for strategic bombing, the Eighth carried through every task of tactical support of the ground forces called for by the Supreme Commander. We helped to cover the Normandy beaches, and later the Dutch airborne landings, with protective air umbrellas. On June 6th, we flew a record-breaking 4,700 sorties. We sealed off the bridgeheads from enemy reserves by cutting the Seine and Loire bridges, and by hammering Nazi communications. Precision bombing blazed the way for the ground forces through enemy strong points. Before D-Day we flew thousands of tons of munitions and equipment to resistance movements on the continent; rushed emergency shipments of food, medical and other vital supplies to ground forces during the crucial month of August; and co-operated in the development of psychological warfare by dropping almost 900,000,000 leaflets in enemy-controlled territory by night, and additional millions during daylight missions.

In air battles during 1944, fighter pilots and bomber crews destroyed over 6,000 enemy aircraft. Strafing attacks by our fighters accounted for 1,950 more. In precision attacks on enemy airfields and factories, our heavies not only blasted production facilities, but also damaged or destroyed an additional 2,630 Nazi aircraft. Fighters also knocked out 3,652 locomotives, 502 freight cars, 3,436 trucks, and significant numbers of tank cars, ammunition dumps and similar ground targets.

Ground crews equalled the fliers in their devotion to duty. Men have frequently worked for 72 hours without rest to put their ships back in the air. There was a steady rise in percentages of aircraft in commission – in spite of growing numbers of sorties monthly and increased battle damage. Just before D-Day, the number of planes to be serviced rose sharply; the job was done with no increase in numbers of ground crews.

Recognition for achievements both in the air and on the ground came to many of you in 1944, in the form of decorations from our Government. Of the five highest and most cherished awards that our country can bestow for valorous conduct, 594 were won by members of the Eighth. Seven of these were Congressional Medals of Honor.

The story of the Eighth is the story of all of you. Together we have become one of the mightiest striking forces of all time. As pioneers of the daylight precision assault, we will continue that assault until final victory is won.

Fighter Statistics and Specifications European Theatre of Operations

Eighth USAAF fighter operations (combat groups) August 1942 through May

Number of days with operations 368.00
Average number of sorties per operational day 628.85
Total sorties flown 261,039
Total sorties less spares and aborts. 257,443
Credit sorties 242,931
Effective sorties 234,393

Aircraft sorties by type of mission

Heavy bomber support 207,857
Strafing and bombing sweeps. 49,586
Number of aircraft dropping bombs. 14,990
Bomb tonnage dropped on targets 4980.7
Aircraft missing in action 2,048

Enemy aircraft claims in the air

Destroyed 5,222
Probably destroyed. 348
Damaged. 1,568

Enemy aircraft claims on the ground

Destroyed 4,250
Probably destroyed. 23
Damaged. 2,886

Eighth USAAF fighter ground claims/ETO February 1944 through April 1945

Target	Destroyed	Damaged	Total
Locomotives	4,660	2,791	7,451
Oil tank cars	1,500	1,422	2,922
Trains	20	226	246
Goods railroad wagons	6,069	23,929	29,998
Armoured vehicles and tanks	178	253	431
Flak towers/gun positions	270	557	827
Motor trucks	3,858	3,091	6,949
Other vehicles	1,021	720	1,741
Tugs, barges, freighters	129	853	982
Railroadstations/facilities	51	234	285
Radio and power stations	102	294	396
Oil storage tanks	73	127	200
Hangars/misc buildings	234	600	834

Eighth USAAF photo and mapping operations 7th photo group March 1943 through April 1945

Total sorties flown 4,593
Total credit sorties 4,247
Effective sorties 3,354
Aircraft losses/missing in action 53
Aircraft category E. 15
Aircraft missing 0
Pilots killed in action 9
Pilots missing in action 46

Photo reconnaissance unit escort 7th photo group January 1945 through April 1945

Total sorties flown 937
Total credit sorties 880
Effective sorties 853
Aircraft losses/missing in action 5
Aircraft category E. 5
Aircraft missing 0
Enemy aircraft claims/destroyed. 0
Enemy aircraft claims/probably destroyed. 1
Enemy aircraft claims/damaged 1

Pilots killed in action 0
pilots missing in action 4

Eighth USAAF fighter aircraft attrition

P-47 Thunderbolt April 1943 through May 1945
Missing in action 529
Category E 176
Missing 44
War weary 176
Non-operational salvage 131
Gains from previous losses 13
Net inventory loss 1,043

P-38 Lightning October 1943 through May 1945
Missing in action 266
Category E 84
Missing 2
War weary 29
Non-operational salvage 74
Gains from previous losses 4
Net inventory loss 451

P-51 Mustang January 1944 through May 1945
Missing in action 1,235
Category E 514
Missing 132
War weary 168
Non-operational salvage 190
Gains from previous losses 38
Net inventory losses 2,201

Eighth USAAF operational definitions

Sortie: A sortie is an aircraft airborne on a mission against the enemy (aircraft dispatched, aircraft airborne, aircraft taking off).

A/C credit sortie: An aircraft credit sortie is deemed to have taken place when an airplane, ordered on an operational mission and in the performance of that mission, has entered an area where enemy anti-aircraft fire may be effective or where usual enemy fighter patrols occur; or when the airplane in any way is subjected to enemy attack.

Effective sortie: A sortie that carries out the purpose of the mission. An aircraft, when loaded with bombs or markers, is considered an effective sortie when it has released one or more armed bombs or markers, either by individually sighting or upon that of the formation leader, such sighting being made with the use of sighting or radar equipment, in a deliberate attempt to destroy or mark a target. Aircraft not loaded with bombs or markers are considered effective sorties if they carry out the purpose of the mission, e.g. drop leaflets, drop chaff, carry out weather flights, take photos, provide escort, carry out diversion as ordered, etc. Lost aircraft, unless definitely known to have been lost before reaching the target, are to be considered as effective sorties.

Non-effective sortie: A sortie that, for any reason, fails to carry out the purpose of the mission.

Missing: If personnel have not returned.

Wounded: Due to enemy action; qualified by such words as 'slightly' or 'seriously'.

Killed: In combat or fatalities when pertaining to aircraft accident deaths.

Injured: Not due to enemy action; qualified by such words as 'slightly' or 'seriously'.

Enemy airplane losses

Destroyed: An enemy aircraft in flight shall be considered destroyed when (1) it is seen to crash, (2) it is seen to disintegrate in the air or to be enveloped in flames, (3) it is seen to descend on friendly territory and be captured, (4) the pilot and entire crew are seen to bale out. An enemy aircraft not in flight shall be considered destroyed when (1) it is seen by photograph to have been blown apart or burnt out, (2) it is seen by strike photo to have been within unobstructed lethal radius of a fragmentation bomb, (3) it is seen to sink in deep water, (4) it is known to have been aboard a carrier or other ship at the time of a confirmed sinking.

Probably destroyed: An aircraft shall be considered probably destroyed when (1) while in flight the enemy airplane is seen to break off combat under circumstances which lead to the conclusion that it must be a loss, although it is not seen to crash, (2) the enemy airplane is so damaged by bombing or strafing as to have less than an even chance of being repaired.

Our aircraft losses

Operational losses
Missing in action: Airplanes which are known to be lost in enemy territory or at sea.

Category E (salvage): An airplane damaged beyond economical repair while engaged in or in performance of an operational mission.

Missing (unknown): Airplanes reported as believed to have landed in friendly territory on the continent, unlocated and/or unheard of during the month of loss or 30 days thereafter (applies only to operations after D-day).

Non-operational losses
War weary: Tactical aircraft that, because of age, obsolescence, excessive repair requirements or other reasons are classified as permanently unfit for combat.

Non-operational salvage: An aircraft damaged beyond economical repair while not in performance of an operational mission (accidents not due to enemy action, training flights, etc).

Other definitions
Mission: Any ordered flight. There are three types of missions.

Service mission: A mission such as ferrying personnel, material or aircraft within or between theaters of operations when no enemy opposition is expected.

Training mission: A mission for training purposes.

Operational mission: An ordered flight with the designed purpose of operating against the enemy.

Encounter: An encounter is deemed to have taken place whenever unfriendly airplanes meet, whether a combat ensues or not.

Combat: Combat is deemed to have taken place whenever contact is made with opposing forces and fire is exchanged or developed by one side or the other.

United States operational fighter aircraft/ETO (principal)

Republic P-47D Thunderbolt. Span = 40′ 9.5″, length = 36′ 1″, height = 14′ 8″. Performance: 433 mph at 30,000 feet, cruise: 210–320 mph, rate of climb: 30,000 feet in 20 minutes. Bomb load: three 1,000-pound or ten 5″

rockets. Power: one Pratt & Whitney R-2800-59 2,000 horsepower radial. Armament: eight .50 caliber wing machine-guns. Range: 590 miles at 25,000 feet or 950 miles with drop tank.

Lockheed P-38 J Lightning. Span = 52', length = 37' 10", height = 9' 10". Performance: 414 mph at 25,000 feet, cruise: 250–320 mph, rate of climb: 30,000 feet in 13.5 minutes. Bomb load: 4,000 pounds or ten 5" rockets. Power: two Allison V-1710-89/91 1,425 horsepower in-lines. Armament: one 20 mm cannon and four .50 caliber machine-guns. Range: 450 miles or 850 miles with drop tanks.

North American P-51B Mustang. Span = 37' length = 32' 3", height = 13' 8". Performance: 440 mph at 30,000 feet, cruise: 210–320 mph, rate of climb: 30,000 feet in 12.5 minutes. Bomb load: two 500-pound. Power: one Packard Merlin V-1650-3 or -7 1,380 horsepower in-line. Armament: four .50 caliber wing machine-guns. Range: 700 miles or 1,500 miles with drop tanks.

North American P-51D Mustang. Span = 37' length = 32' 3", height = 13' 8". Performance: 437 mph at 25,000 feet, cruise: 210–320 mph, rate of climb: 30,000 feet in 13 minutes. Power: one Packard Merlin V-1650-7 1,490 horsepower in-line. Armament: six .50 caliber wing machine-guns. Range: 700 miles or 1,500 miles with drop tanks.

United States operational fighter aircraft/ETO (additional)

Vickers-Supermarine Spitfire VB. Span = 36' 10", length = 29' 11", height = 12' 7". Performance: 369 mph at 19,500 feet, cruise: 270 mph at 5,000 feet, rate of climb: 4,750 feet per minute. Power: one Rolls-Royce Merlin 45, 1,470 horsepower in-line. Armament: two 20 mm cannon and four .303 wing machine-guns. Range: 395 miles.

Vickers-Supermarine Spitfire IX. Span = 36' 10", length = 31' 4", height = 12' 7.25". Performance: 408 mph at 25,000 feet, cruise: 325 mph at 20,000 feet, rate of climb: 4,100 feet per minute. Bomb load: 750 pounds. Power: one Rolls-Royce Merlin 61, 1,565 horsepower in-line. Armament: two 20 mm cannon and two .50 caliber wing machine-guns. Range: 235 miles.

Vickers-Supermarine Spitfire XI (pr). Span = 36' 10", length = 31' 4.5", height = 12' 7.25". Performance: 422 mph at 27,500 feet, cruise: 340 mph at 20,000 feet, rate of climb: 4,350 feet per minute. Power: one Rolls-Royce Merlin 63 or 70, 1,640 horsepower in-line. Range: 1,360 miles.

German operational fighter aircraft/ETO (principal)

Focke Wulf Fw 190. Span = 34′ 6″, length = 29′ 7″, height = 13′. Performance: 408 mph at 15,750 feet, cruise: 296 mph, rate of climb: 20,000 feet in 9.1 minutes. Bomb load: 1,100 pounds. Power: one BMW 801 1,700 horsepower radial. Armament: four 20 mm and two 13 mm cannon. Range: 525 miles.

Messerschmttt Bf 109. Span = 32′ 6.5″, length = 29′ 4″, height = 8′ 6″. Performance: 452 mph at 19,685 feet, cruise: 310 mph, rate of climb: 16,400 feet in 3 minutes. Bomb load: 1,200 pounds. Power: one Daimler Benz 605 1,500 horsepower in-line. Armament: one 30 mm and two 15 mm cannon. Range: 440 miles.

Messerschmitt Bf 110. Span = 53′ 5″, length = 41′ 7″, height = 13′ 1″. Performance: 342 mph at 22,900 feet, cruise: 200 mph, rate of climb: 18,000 feet in 7.9 minutes. Bomb load: 2,000 pounds. Power: two Daimler Benz 1,475 horsepower (each) in-line. Armament: two 30 mm and two 20 mm cannon, and two 7.92 mm machine-guns. Range: 1,305 miles.

German operational fighter aircraft/ETO (additional)

Messerschmitt Me 262 Schwalbe. Span = 40′ 11.5″, length = 34′ 9.5″, height = 12′ 7″.Performance: 540 mph at 19,700 feet, cruise: unknown, rate of climb: 3,900 feet (initial). Bomb load: 1,100 pounds. Power: two Junkers Jumo 1,980 pounds thrust (each). Armament: four 30 mm cannon and twenty-four 50 mm rockets. Range: 652 miles at 30,000 feet.

Messerschmitt Me 163B-1A Komet. Span = 30′ 7.3″, length = 19′ 2.3″, height = 9′. Performance: 596 mph between 9,800 feet and 29,500 feet, rate of climb: 29,500 feet in 2 minutes 36 seconds. Power: one Walter Hawk 509A-2 rocket 3,748 pounds thrust. Armament: two 30 mm cannon. Maximum endurance: 7.5 minutes.

British operational fighter aircraft/ETO (principal)

Hawker Hurricane IIB. Span = 40′, length = 32′ 3″, height = 13′ 1.5″. Performance: 340 mph at 21,000 feet, cruise: 307 mph, rate of climb: 20,000 feet in 7.5 minutes. Bomb load: 1,000 pounds or eight rockets. Power: one Rolls-Royce Merlin XX 1,280 horsepower in-line. Armament: six, eight or twelve .303 wing machine-guns. Range: 985 miles with external tanks or 480 miles without tanks.

Vickers-Supermarine Spitfire 1A. Span = 36′ 10″, length = 29′ 11″, height: 8′ 10″. Performance: 362 mph at 19,000 feet, cruise: 315 mph at 20,000 feet, rate of climb: 20,000 feet in 9.5 minutes. Power: one Rolls-Royce Merlin III 1,030 horsepower in-line. Armament: eight .303 machine-guns. Range: 395 miles.

Vickers-Supermarine Spitfire IX. Span = 36' 10", length = 31' 4", height = 12' 7.25". Performance: 408 mph at 25,000 feet, cruise: 325 mph at 20,000 feet, rate of climb: 4,100 feet per minute. Bomb load: 750 pounds. Power: one Rolls-Royce Merlin 61 1,565 horsepower in-line. Armament: two 20 mm cannon and two .50 caliber wing machine-guns. Range: 235 miles.

Vickers-Supermarine Spitfire IXE. Span = 36' 10", length = 31' 4", height = 12' 7.25". Performance: 416 mph at 27,500 feet, cruise: 322 mph, rate of climb: 20,000 feet in 6.4 minutes. Bomb load: 750 pounds. Power: one Rolls-Royce Merlin 70 1,710 horsepower in-line. Armament: two 20 mm cannon and two .50 caliber wing machine-guns. Range: 980 miles with external tanks or 430 miles without tanks.

Vickers-Supermarine Spitfire XIVE. Span = 36' 10", length = 32' 8", height = 12' 8.5". Performance: 448 mph at 26,000 feet, 363 mph at 20,000 feet, rate of climb: 20,000 feet in 7 minutes. Bomb load: 1,000 pounds. Power: one Rolls-Royce Griffon 65 2,050 horsepower in-line. Armament: two 20 mm cannon and two .50 caliber wing machine-guns. Range: 460 miles or 850 miles with drop tanks.

Hawker Hurricane I. Span = 40', length = 31' 4", height = 13' 1.5". Performance: 328 mph at 20,000 feet, cruise: unknown, rate of climb: 20,000 feet in 8.5 minutes. Power: one Rolls-Royce Merlin III 1,030 horse-power in-line. Armament: eight .303 wing machine-guns. Range: 425 miles.

Hawker Typhoon 1B. Span = 41' 7", length = 31' 11.5", height = 15' 4". Performance: 414 mph at 11,500 feet, cruise: 330 mph, rate of climb: 15,000 feet in 5 minutes 50 seconds. Bomb load: 2,000 pounds or eight 60 pound rockets. Power: one Napier Sabre IIC 2,200 horsepower in-line. Armament: four 20 mm cannon. Range: 740 miles or 1,530 miles with drop tanks.

Hawker Tempest V. Span = 41', length = 33' 8", height = 16' 1". Perform-ance: 436 mph at 15,000 feet, cruise: 391 mph at 18,800 feet, rate of climb: 15,000 feet in 5 minutes. Bomb load: 2,000 pounds. Power: one Napier Sabre IIV, -B or -C 2,180, 2,200 or 2,260 horse-power in-line. Armament: four 20 mm cannon. Range: 740 miles or 1,530 miles with drop tanks.

Index